OFFICIAL

RI∨EN™

THE SEQUEL TO MYST®

HINTS AND SOLUTIONS

by William H. Keith, Jr. and Nina Barton

||||BradyGAMES
STRATEGY GUIDES

Legal Stuff

Brady Publishing
An Imprint of
Macmillan Computer Publishing USA
201 West 103rd Street
Indianapolis, Indiana 46290

ISBN: 1-56686-709-6

Library of Congress Catalog #: 97-073740

Printing Code: The rightmost double-digit number is the year of the book's printing; the rightmost single-digit number is the number of the book's printing. For example, 97-1 shows that the first printing of the book occurred in 1997.

99 98 97   3 2

Manufactured in the United States of America.

Brady Staff

Publisher
Lynn Zingraf

Editor In Chief
H. Leigh Davis

Licensing Manager
David Waybright

Marketing Manager
Janet Cadoff

Acquisitions Editor
Debra McBride

Credits

Project Editor
Tim Cox

Screenshot Editor
Michael Owen

Designer
Cyan®

Production Designers
Dan Caparo
Joe Millay
Max Adamson

TABLE OF CONTENTS

Author Acknolwedgements

Any game guide like this one is of necessity a collaborative effort by many people. We would like to extend our special thanks, however, to Tim Cox, our editor at BradyGAMES, and to Brady's Acquisitions Editor Debra McBride, who made it all both possible and worthwhile.

Of course, there would be no game guide without the game, or the talented team of programmers and developers who put it together, but we would like to especially thank our guides through Cyan's land of Riven, Robyn Miller, Rich Watson, and Bonnie Staub.

And finally, our very special and sincere thanks to Cyan's Chris Brandkamp, who opened to us the mystical and wonderful universe that is Riven.

Author Bios

William H. Keith, Jr.

As of this writing, Bill has written over 50 books and has several more in the pipeline, novels ranging from military technothrillers to military science fiction to science fiction comedy. Current series include *Warstrider*, an SF series under his own name, and *SEALs: The Warrior Breed*, a military historical-fiction series under the pseudonym H. Jay Riker. Before he started writing for a living, he was a professional SF illustrator and still occasionally exhibits his work at various cons and on the World Wide Web.

When he's not writing—*is* there such a time?—he can be found hiking, blowing holes in paper targets with firearms of various calibers, participating in Western Pennsylvania Mensa events, and hanging out with some very strange people. He lives in the mountains of western Pennsylvania with his wife, Nina.

Nina Barton

After years of editing Bill's prolific output, Nina Barton—alias Nina Keith—has begun writing on her own, probably out of sheer self defense. Unlike Bill, she understands both computers and computer people, a highly desirable talent when working on a computer game guide for BradyGAMES.

She is currently co-writing several novels with Bill. When she's able to pry herself away from the computer, she likes to hike, go to concerts, teach piano, shoot things, go to Mensa conventions, and hang around in bookstores. She lives with Bill in western Pennsylvania.

This is Bill and Nina's fifth book for BradyGAMES.

INTRODUCTION

Sunlight dances off an azure sea. You hear the cry of wheeling gulls overhead, the buzz and click of insects in the verdant forest growth. You stand alone on the rocky shore of an island where, in the distance, you see strange and wonderful devices luring you forward with the promise of mystery and wonder. It has been long since you unlocked the puzzles of Myst Island and freed Atrus from the prison of dark and labyrinthine D'ni. A new test and new challenges await you now.

Welcome to the Fifth Age and the mysterious world of Riven.

Riven is a complex and challenging game, replete with puzzles of devious and almost diabolical cunning. *Official Riven Solutions* strategy guide is designed to enable you to work your way through each location within the Fifth Age and make decisions for yourself. Do I want a word or two to push me in the right direction? Or, do I want a step-by-step listing of the places I must go and the things I must do to crack each puzzle in turn?

Vague to Specific: How Much Do You Want To Know?

Each chapter of this book is rated according to how little or how much it actually gives away. To understand the graphic symbols that warn of spoilers to the game, however, you'll need to take a quick look at a few of the creatures that inhabit the islands of Riven.

The Beetle

This is a small and harmless creature you may see flying around in the jungle or crawling on a log.

A beetle at the head of a chapter means that very little is given away in that section. There are no hints or solutions of any kind, although some of the background information may be generally useful in your quest.

The Frog

You may or may not see a frog
in your wanderings. Frogs are
harmless, but they're a step up
on the food chain from beetles.

A frog at the head of a chapter means that the
section in question does contain hints, although
no solutions are given away outright. Refer to
these sections for subtle hints or a gentle nudge
in the right direction.

The Sunner

You may, if you're lucky,
encounter sunners in Riven.
Sunners are bizarre, otherworld-
ly creatures that resemble
improbable hybrids of penguins, baleen whales,
and plesiosaurs. Sunners are decidedly larger
than frogs and much more mysterious.

A Sunner indicates that the section gives away
quite a bit. It will stop short of telling you the
solutions to the puzzles outright, but it will
take you to the very brink of revelation. If
you'd rather figure out the puzzles for yourself,
don't look in these chapters!

The Wahrk

You may never encounter one in your travels, but signs of the wahrk's existence—and its importance to the world-islands  of Riven—are everywhere. It is an aquatic beast, a melding of whale and shark, and it is undeniably dangerous.

The wahrk icon is reserved for those sections that give away everything. If you want to preserve any of the mystery and brain-teasing wonder of Riven and you come to this symbol, do not read any further!

CHAPTER BY CHAPTER

Official Riven Solutions

Now that you've completed your lesson in Riven zoology, let's look at how the chapters of this book are organized.

INTRODUCTION

This introduction to the game and the book gives away nothing of substance. It includes this description of the book's chapters and a section on how to use this book.

CHAPTER 1: Roaming Through Riven

This is a brief chapter that, again, gives away very little. It provides a quick look at the game controls and cursor types, and a brief overview of how to maneuver through the worlds of Riven.

CHAPTER 2: The Islands of Riven: Maps and Specifics

This chapter is divided into sections describing each area within Riven. Each area is mapped out in detail; for example, looking at a map of Jungle Island will definitely give away some of the surprises, if only because you will know what's on the other side of that tunnel or which direction on a forking path to choose in order to reach a particular control. Also included are lists of the puzzles and problems that must be solved in order for you to proceed through the game, along with some specific hints and tips for solving them.

Use this chapter carefully if you want to preserve the mystery and suspense of the rest of the game!

CHAPTER 3: Puzzles and Problems: The Solutions

The Gate Room. The Gallows. The Star Fissure Window. This chapter lists each of the major puzzles and problems in the game and tells you how to solve  them. Remember, though, that much of the pleasure of playing Riven comes from piecing together the subtle and widely scattered clues that enable you to reason out the answers for yourself. Please don't look in this chapter unless you're totally baffled and cannot solve the problem in any other way!

CHAPTER 4: Walkthrough: All Revealed

This is the spoiler chapter, the one that gives away everything. It takes you step-by-step through the entire game, solving  each puzzle and showing you exactly what to do to get from the beginning to the end, assuming no missed steps and virtual clairvoyance on the part of the player. At the end of the chapter, you will find brief descriptions of the several alternate endings to the Riven saga.

"Walkthrough: All Revealed" will actually prove to be most useful to you after you've completed the game, because it will help you piece together everything and see how it all works and how you might have done things differently. Do *not* read this chapter if you want a chance to work things out for yourself!

APPENDIX A: How It All Came To Be

This relatively brief narrative, gleaned from the journals and dialogues of the various characters in Riven, provides a detailed look at the backstory of Riven. It details who constructed what, and why and what it has to do with the story line of the game. This appendix does not give any specific puzzle solutions, but it does assume that you have completed the game and know all of the secrets, which it may refer to in passing. If you would rather learn about some important revelations in the game as you play, don't read this section.

APPENDIX B: Worlds for the Making

Did you know that merely observing something might be necessary for that something's very existence? That describing a world—or a universe—might actually call it into being? A brief essay on the bizarre and real (whatever that means!) world of quantum mechanics, on the multiplicity of alternate universes, and on the probable realities of Riven. This section refers to specific locations and personalities within the game only in passing and gives away nothing important.

Using Official Riven Solutions

Perhaps you've just purchased Riven and are wondering how to start. More likely, you've played through the game until you encountered a deviously twisted puzzle which, after hours of play, thought, and head-scratching, you cannot solve. Or, possibly, you've only heard about Riven and are reading this book to get an idea as to whether you really want to lose yourself in this fascinating, alternate reality.

Wherever you're coming from, you decide how much you want the writers of this book to tell you. Read the section in this chapter entitled "Vague to Specific: How Much Do You Want To Know?" to learn about the four symbols that represent the "level of spoiler" provided by each chapter.

If all you want is a general overview of the game mechanics (what the different cursors are and how to move around) read Chapter 1, "Roaming  Through Riven." There are also some very general suggestions regarding gameplay, or things to keep in mind as you move from to place to place.

Even with all of our carefully worded hints, the twisted cunning of a particular puzzle or set of clues is just too much. What you need is straight talk about how to solve a particular problem, but without having the answer handed to you on a platter. If you want to see maps of the various locations, or would like a list of the puzzles and problems you must solve in each location with some hints on how to go about it, read Chapter 2, "The Islands of Riven: Maps and Specifics." If you would prefer to read a narrative about Riven's backstory, which describes what the different locations and puzzles mean and what they're all about, read Appendix A, "How It All Came To Be."

Okay, okay! Enough hints, vague suggestions, and cute stuff! If you read the words "Have you checked the entire room carefully for clues?" just one more time, you're going to commit cybercide! You're up against a steel-plated wall, and there is no way you're going to solve this puzzle in any time less than a decade or two.

If you want the specific solutions to each of Riven's puzzles and step-by-step revelations describing how each problem can be solved, read Chapter 3,
"Puzzles and Problems: The Solutions." If you would rather see a walkthrough that reveals

everything, taking you from start to finish in the shortest possible time, go to Chapter 4, "Walkthrough: All Revealed." This chapter takes you through all of Riven by the most direct path possible, but be warned that you will lose most of the flavor and enjoyment of the game this way. Chapter 4 is best used after you've already successfully completed the game as a way of checking how well you did, or to see how else the game might have ended.

And finally, before you begin, here is one free piece of advice for playing Riven. Take your time! Enjoy and savor each location. Live it. Think about it. Turn it around in your mind. Take the time to puzzle each mystery out, rather than reaching for this book each time you face a problem that, at first glance, appears insoluble.

Riven is a universe of startling complexity, realism, consistency, and thoughtfulness. Some of the problems are extraordinarily difficult, but you can work them out if you think them through. There are no time limits, but there is a universe of satisfaction that comes with each successful solution, each mastered clue, each correct assumption, each completed link.

Enjoy!

CHAPTER ONE
Roaming Through Riven

Unlike so many other CD-ROM games, Riven
has a player interface that is simple, direct, and
natural, almost as though you're physically in
the world you are exploring. Getting around is
literally a matter of pointing and clicking.
Notice the hand-shaped cursor on your screen?
The appearance of the cursor changes depending on the actions that are available to you.

To Walk Forward

Move the pointing cursor to the spot
on the path to which you want to go
and then click. The view on your screen
will change to reflect your changed point of

view. Sometimes you will need to click on a
particular part of the screen in order to move
forward. Note that there will be times when it
is simply not possible to move any farther. If
clicking on the view ahead has no effect, turn
left or right or try looking up or down to
locate another route.

To Take a Left or Right Path

As you approach an intersection, you can
choose which path to take by moving the forward cursor over the desired path and clicking.
With sharp turns, you may need to move
abreast of the intersection, turn, and then move
forward as you normally would.

Turn Left/Right

Move the cursor to the left or right side
of the screen until you see it point in the
indicated direction. Click and your point of
view will rotate 90 degrees.

Turn Around

In open spaces, turn left or right twice to
turn yourself around and face back the
way you came. In close quarters (for
example, a cavern, or a tunnel), the left- or
right-pointing finger will appear crooked, as
though pointing back over your shoulder.

Clicking when you see this cursor appear turns you 180 degrees.

Look Up/Move Up

Move the cursor to the top of the screen. If the up-pointing hand changes from palm away from you to palm facing you, so that you can see the fingers, clicking the mouse will enable you to look or move in the direction in which the hand is pointing. Note that it is not always possible to look or move up.

Look Down/Move Down/Move Back

Move the cursor to the bottom of the screen. When the cursor changes to a down-pointing hand, clicking enables you to look down (over the edge of a cliff, for example), move down (descend a ladder), or move back (retreat from a close-up view). Note that these actions are not always possible.

Push/Pick Up/Handle/Manipulate

Keep an eye on your cursor. If there is something on your screen that can be manipulated (for example, a switch that can be thrown), you will see the icon change to an open hand. Click or click and drag to manipulate the object.

Zip

When the Zip feature is selected in the menu bar, the cursor may change into a small lightning bolt when it is moved to a particular area of the landscape. If you see the lightning bolt, you can zip directly to that location. This is a great time saver; it prevents a lot of trekking back and forth. Just remember that there's a lot to be learned from the landscape—don't miss it all in the rush!

The world of Riven is there for you to explore. Experiment! Try everything! You will very soon find that the cursor controls are second nature. Just remember: If something doesn't work, try something else. There's got to be a way to get to where you're going!

General Hints for Exploring Riven

There are a few very general hints that you should follow when playing Riven. These are things to keep in mind as you explore the complex, beautiful, and fascinating world of Riven.

Examine Everything

There are numerous objects in Riven that provide you with a closer look at items. Click on them to get a better view. Some devices enable you to further manipulate them by opening them or turning them on, which may prove to be important. Play with everything and note the results. Several devices have eyepieces, peep-holes, or image viewing areas that require an up-close peek. Click on them to have a look.

Have a Look Around

The panoramas of the Riven sea and landscapes are breathtakingly spectacular. Stop frequently and take a careful look around. Admire the scenery, but also search for geographical clues. Try to orient yourself in the landscape, and be especially aware of the various buildings and structures and how they're sited on the various islands. You will need to pick up on such geographical clues as the location of certain bridges, where they lead to, whether they're open or closed, and so on.

If In Doubt, Turn It On

Try everything, throw every switch, pull every lever, and note the results. There are some mechanisms in Riven that must be set in a particular combination with other mechanisms, or which must be turned off so something else can be turned on. In general, it's in your best interests to turn on everything.

Understand the Mechanisms

You will encounter numerous mechanisms in Riven, strange devices that you must manipulate to open, move, look into, or turn on. Examine all such machines carefully by moving the cursor all over them to check for areas that seem to enable you to manipulate them in some way. Then click and drag on the various controls. Try different combinations. Try to understand what the thing does and what it's used for. There may be subtle clues—a new

sound or a change in some part of the landscape around you. Try to pick up on these clues
and piece them together to form a picture of
how the machine works and why.

Be Systematic

One lever may turn the power on or off for a
number of locations, depending on how it is
set. You may need to experiment by throwing
the lever to one position, and then moving
around and observing things to see what was
turned on and what was turned off before
returning and trying it in a different position.

Be Observant

Nothing in Riven was placed without a reason.
Note such relatively minor details as where a
steam pipe vanishes into the rock and try to
determine where that same pipe emerges on
the other side. Discover what it's connected to
and you might figure out what it's for! Be
aware, too, of the sounds you hear. A few will
be important enough that you will want to
take note of them, so that you can remember
them later.

Be Persistent

Some puzzles may take many, many attempts
before you crack it. Some will require you to
travel back and forth between widely separated

parts of an island, or even between several different islands, before you've assembled all of the necessary clues. You may notice something new about a scene each time you go there. Keep at it!

Read the Journals

Atrus gives you his journal at the beginning of the game. Later, you may be able to acquire or read the journals kept by Catherine and Gehn. Read them! They are not there solely as background or atmosphere. There may be specific clues—even codes or the solutions to specific puzzles—hidden within these pages.

Keep a Notebook

Don't trust your memory, especially if gameplay is going to extend over a period of weeks or months! During your explorations, you will be required to learn certain symbols and relate those symbols to other things. When you see a symbol that is obviously intended as something more than decoration, copy it down. You will probably need it later!

Make Maps

Veteran game players don't need the following advice: Make maps of your journeys, and note what you find at different points along the way. Chapter 2 of this guide includes maps of all of your destinations, but the thrill of discovery and the satisfaction of a deduction confirmed is much richer if you keep that chapter closed for the time being and draw your own maps as you explore. There are important clues in the relationships of certain structures, one with another, and the function of some controls can be inferred by noting the existence of pipe or walkway connections.

Keep a Journal

Atrus, Gehn, and Catherine all keep journals of their experiments, thoughts, and decisions. Shouldn't you? Some puzzle solutions require careful thought and the accumulation of clues from widely diverse locales. Many clues you acquire won't be needed until late in the game, when the larger picture finally begins to make sense. A journal of your thoughts, musings, and speculations might help you pick up on subtle, but necessary, clues.

Save Frequently

Here's another piece of advice that veteran gamers recognize: Save often! This adventure requires a lot of traveling to work out the various puzzles and problems. It would be a real shame if you were almost all the way through, and then discovered that you'd made a mistake or a rash assumption and had to return to the beginning to retrace your steps!

In general, save your game before traveling to another island or before getting too deeply involved in a new puzzle. That way, if things go wrong, you can restore your game from your last save, instead of repeating the whole thing.

Take Your Time!

Riven is an extraordinarily rich and complex world. You are under no time restraints and you are not in a race. Take your time and enjoy the experience! It may take you several gaming sessions to crack a particular puzzle, numerous restores from saved games, and many different approaches to find the right sequence or code.

And remember! If things get too impossible, well, that's why you have this guide book, isn't it?

CHAPTER TWO
The Islands of Riven:
Maps and Specifics

This is a Sunner chapter. It contains both hints and tips for playing the game, and specific hints for solving certain key puzzles. Reading this chapter before playing Riven will rob the game of some of its fun and suspense.

This chapter is divided into sections that describe each area within Riven. This chapter maps out each area in detail. You can use these maps to determine where you are, where you've been, and where you want to go, but you'll definitely lose some of the mystery and suspense along the way.

Also included in this chapter are lists of the puzzles and problems that must be solved in order for you to proceed through the game, along with some specific hints and tips for solving them. It stops short of giving away the entire solution to each problem, but it definitely gives away an awful lot!

Temple Island

You start your adventure on Temple Island, south of the Star Fissure and the Telescope. You must untangle the mysteries of the Gate Room, the Great Golden Dome, and the Temple.

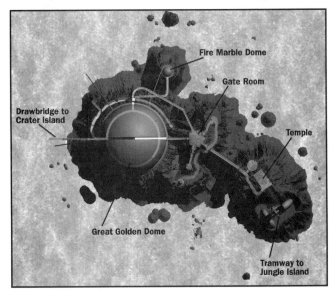

Fire Marble Dome

Gate Room

Drawbridge to Crater Island

Temple

Great Golden Dome

Tramway to Jungle Island

Puzzles and Problems on Temple Island

▶ Solve the puzzle of the Gate Room. How do you get where you need to go and open the gates and grates you need to open?

▶ Provide power to the telescope.

▶ How do you reach the Golden Dome?

▶ What can you turn on in the Golden Dome?

▶ The Fire Marble Dome Puzzle. How do you open it? What symbol is associated with it?

▶ The Temple. What can you learn about its designer? How do you open the outer Temple door?

After completing your initial explorations of Temple Island, you should have:

▶ Figured out how to use the Gate Room to access any of the five doors.

▶ Lowered the grates that block two of the doors.

▶ Turned on the power to the telescope.

▶ Explored the Golden Dome and switched on power to the West Drawbridge to Crater Island and the drawbridge between the Gate Room and the Golden Dome.

▶ Opened the main door of the Temple and found the Tram to Jungle Island.

You may also have seen the Temple Island Fire Marble Dome, but you can only open it on a later visit.

Puzzles and Problems on Jungle Island

Ride the mag-lev tram from Temple Island to Jungle Island. This area is larger and has a lot more in the way of secrets and mysteries than did Temple Island.

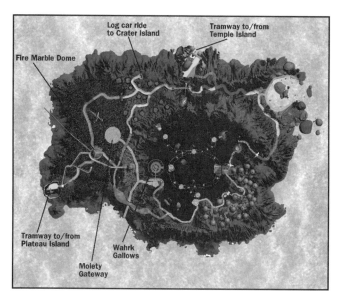

Log car ride
to Crater Island

Tramway to/from
Temple Island

Fire Marble Dome

Tramway to/from
Plateau Island

Wahrk
Gallows

Molety
Gateway

▶ What is the purpose of the wooden eyes?

▶ Can you link each eye with a particular animal, through a particular sound the animal makes and/or through the silhouette of that animal?

▶ Can you find four wooden eyes?

▶ Can you find a place where you can learn the meaning of the symbols on the back of each wooden eye?

▶ Figure out how to lower the submarine. Then learn how to operate it to travel around Village Lake.

▶ The Control Room: Can you find a way to lower three of the five ladders to gain access to key landings around the inside of Village Lake?

▶ The School Room: Can you learn what you need to know about D'ni numbers?

▶ The Wahrk Gallows: You must close the central opening on the Wahrk Gallows before you can explore all of its secrets.

▶ What is the secret of the Wahrk Idol in the jungle? Can you find a way to reach the catwalks you can see among the trees or the Fire Marble Dome you see turning above you?

▶ There is actually more than one way to reach the Fire Marble Dome. When you do reach it, can you stop the turning and learn the symbol associated with it?

▶ After penetrating the Wahrk Idol's secret, can you find Gehn's raised throne? What can you do there that you must do to continue your explorations?

▶ Back to the Wahrk Gallows: After closing the central opening, can you find the prison holding cell and the secret beyond it? Do you have all of the information you need to solve the Puzzle of the Twenty-five Stones?

▶ Can you find the log-car ride that carries you from Jungle Island to Crater Island? (This one's easy—almost as easy as falling off a log!)

After you've explored Jungle Island, you should have:

▶ Collected four symbols from four wooden eyes and determined what the symbols mean. This is necessary to solve the puzzle of the gateway to the Moiety Age.

▶ Used the submarine to complete a circuit of the lake. You may not have been able to access the Wahrk Gallows the first time around, but you should have reached the Control Tower to lower the ladders, and entered the school room to discover what there is to be learned there.

▶ Found the Wahrk Idol. You may have learned its secret the first time around, or you may need to come back to Jungle Island later from an unexpected direction.

▶ Now, or later, you will need to reach the Jungle Island Fire Marble Dome, learn the appropriate symbol, and visit Gehn's throne. You must reach Gehn's throne to gain access to the Wahrk Gallows.

▶ Once you have access to the Wahrk Gallows, you can find Gehn's prison, solve the problem of finding the gateway to the Moiety Age, and at least begin thinking about how to solve that devious puzzle.

Puzzles and Problems on Crater Island

You ride the log car to another island, this one known as Crater Island. You arrive rather unceremoniously, dumped down a chute and dropped into a chipper that, fortunately for you, is unpowered at the moment.

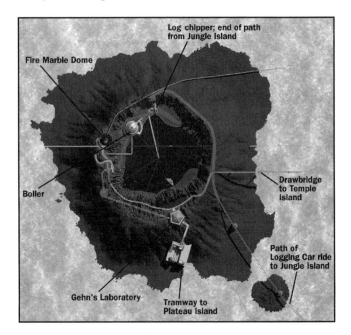

Log chipper; end of path from Jungle Island

Fire Marble Dome

Boiler

Drawbridge to Temple Island

Path of Logging Car ride to Jungle Island

Gehn's Laboratory

Tramway to Plateau Island

▶ Can you solve the puzzle of the boiler? To reach the ladder and passageway in the center of the room beyond the door, you must raise the floor grating, ensuring that the tank is drained of water and that the furnace is off. How do you go about doing this?

▶ After raising the grating and crossing the drainage pipe in the middle of the boiler tank, you can take a long, dark crawl and climb that will deposit you high atop the mountains surrounding the lake. Can you find a path leading over the crest of the ridge and down to a railed balcony?

▶ The apparatus at the end of the long catwalk leading into the mountain is for catching frogs. Can you catch one using the trap and the bait?

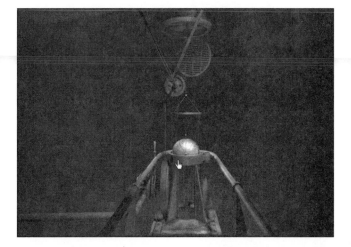

▶ The large building visible on the side of the cliff is Gehn's book-making laboratory. The only door you can reach is locked. Getting in is a problem; it requires an approach from an unexpected direction.

▶ The double doors above the railed balcony on the cliff lead to the frog-catching apparatus, but there's more to this site than meets the eye. Can you find the Fire Marble Dome for Crater Island, and can you find the hidden kinetoscope that stops it?

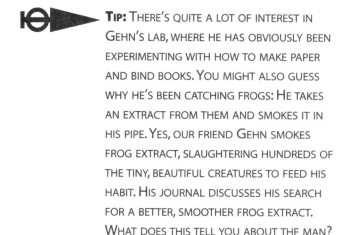

TIP: THERE'S QUITE A LOT OF INTEREST IN GEHN'S LAB, WHERE HE HAS OBVIOUSLY BEEN EXPERIMENTING WITH HOW TO MAKE PAPER AND BIND BOOKS. YOU MIGHT ALSO GUESS WHY HE'S BEEN CATCHING FROGS: HE TAKES AN EXTRACT FROM THEM AND SMOKES IT IN HIS PIPE. YES, OUR FRIEND GEHN SMOKES FROG EXTRACT, SLAUGHTERING HUNDREDS OF THE TINY, BEAUTIFUL CREATURES TO FEED HIS HABIT. HIS JOURNAL DISCUSSES HIS SEARCH FOR A BETTER, SMOOTHER FROG EXTRACT. WHAT DOES THIS TELL YOU ABOUT THE MAN?

After penetrating Gehn's laboratory, you'll gain access to an important source of additional clues that you'll need in your quest. Also, the path is open that leads back to the Golden Dome via the bridge, or you can return to Jungle Island on the log cart, or you can summon a tram from the front of Gehn's lab.

After completing your explorations of Crater Island, you should have:

▶ Solved the puzzles of the boiler, the central power valve, and the ventilation fan duct.

▶ Discovered the location of this island's Fire Marble Dome.

▶ Found and read Gehn's lab journal.

82.2.13 The latest Ink formulation has proven a failure. Even when writing in my most promising Books I obtain only the barest glimmer of a connection. It is frustrating to expend as much effort creating a blank Book, only to end up destroying it when a flaw is detected; there are days when the lab is uncomfortably warm from the flames of these failed attempts. Yet the further I refine each element — the formulations of the inks and papers, the physical dimensions of the Books — the more I realize that the list of potential combinations is nearly infinite. Without access to D'ni I fear that my long term efforts may be greatly hindered. Nevertheless there are avenues of research which remain to be explored.

▶ Found in Gehn's lab journal a series of D'ni numbers.

▶ Found the catwalk and bridge leading back to the Great Golden Dome on Temple Island.

▶ Found the tram outside Gehn's lab.

▶ Learned quite a lot about Gehn and his personal habits.

The tram takes you to the next unexplored island, Plateau Island.

Puzzles and Problems on Plateau Island

The tram from Gehn's lab deposits you on Plateau Island. Note that, while you can get out on the left side of the tram, there is a door visible to the right. Take the left-hand side for now, but keep thinking about how you can gain across to the other side of the tram line.

Plateau Island contains some of the grandest and most spectacular scenery yet seen in the world of Riven. It also holds the key to the most fiendish of Riven's puzzles.

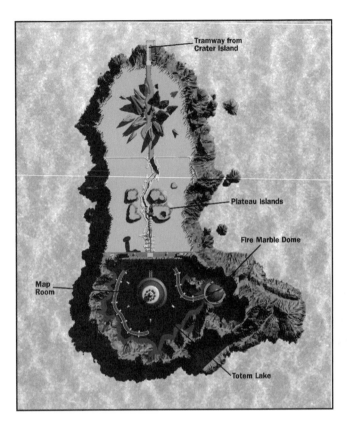

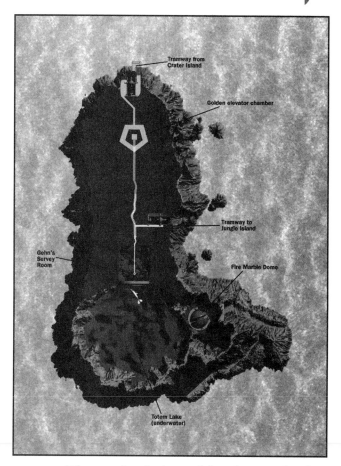

Tramway from
Crater Island

Golden elevator chamber

Tramway to
Jungle Island

Gehn's
Survey
Room

Fire Marble Dome

Totem Lake
(underwater)

▶ The overhead view of the plateau islands
and the corresponding 3-D relief views of
each sector of each island in the Map
Room together constitute both problem
and puzzle. What are you supposed to do
with the information displayed here?

▶ This island's Fire Marble Dome is visible beyond a cleft in the rock wall just past the lake on which the Map Room rests. The kinetoscope, when you find it, is broken. Can you open the dome anyway?

▶ Can you figure out how to reach the other side of the tram?

▶ The Viewing Chamber Puzzles. When you reach the other side, you will encounter one of Gehn's scribes, and, if you pursue him, you will watch him vanish into another tram car—but not the one you arrived in. The passageway beyond the tram car station, however, leads to an underwater viewing chamber that offers several important clues to several of Riven's other puzzles. Can you find them?

When you've finished with Plateau Island, you should:

▶ Have a good guess as to the identity of the fifth animal shape, which will let you solve the Moiety Puzzle on Jungle Island.

▶ Have noted the Fire Marble symbols and matched most of them with a different color. This will help you solve the Gehn's Age Puzzle.

▶ Have learned which patterns of squares represent which islands.

▶ Have solved the Map Puzzle and identified which sector on each island holds a Fire Marble Dome. This, too, is necessary for the solution to the puzzle of Gehn's Age.

▶ Taken the newly discovered tram back to Jungle Island and learned the Wahrk Idol's secret, if you didn't find it earlier.

Puzzles and Problems of Reaching the Moiety Age

You reach the Moiety Age from Jungle Island. When you arrive, a woman named Nelah gives you Catherine's journal and the Trap Book that was taken from you at the beginning of your quest.

Collecting all of the clues you need, however, is a bit of a chore.

▶ Can you solve the problem of finding the gateway to the Moiety Age? You need to learn how to use the submarine to reach the Wahrk Gallows. You also need to have found Gehn's Throne and learned how to close the base of the gallows. Then you must find your way up the gallows to the prison cell, learn the cell's secret, find your way through the darkness, learn how to light your way back, and finally (!) discover the doorway to the gateway.

▶ After finding the gateway, you must know the code for opening it. You must have found and examined four wooden eyes at various points in Jungle Island, and associated each with a particular animal silhouette or, in one case, with the call of an animal that you have seen on the island. You must have associated each animal with a symbol which, at the school room, you've discovered is a number.

▶ With four animals and four numbers, you're almost there, but you also need to discover what the fifth animal silhouette is—the one in the underwater viewing

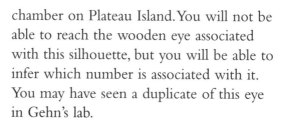

chamber on Plateau Island. You will not be able to reach the wooden eye associated with this silhouette, but you will be able to infer which number is associated with it. You may have seen a duplicate of this eye in Gehn's lab.

▶ Finally, you must touch the proper stones in the gateway room in the proper order. The order is obvious, based on the number associated with each silhouette. If you get the order or the animal graphic wrong, nothing will happen and you must reset the stones by touching each in reverse order or by pressing a sixth stone. When you have the stones in the correct order, the water that covers the far wall will flow away through side channels, the dagger panel will open, enabling you to reach a linking book that will take you to the Moiety Age.

You will be knocked unconscious by a rebel blowgun dart, awakening in a small chamber. At this point, all you need to do is guess what the woman is telling you to do, and do it.

After finishing the Rebel Age, you should have:

▶ The Trap Book taken from you at the beginning of the quest.

▶ Catherine's journal, which contains information you will need later.

The woman will return with another linking book. Touch the image on the book, and you will be returned to the Room of the Twenty-five Stones on Jungle Island.

Puzzles and Problems of Reaching Gehn's Age

Reaching the alternate reality where Gehn lives when he is not playing god and lording it over the inhabitants of Riven involves some of the toughest puzzles in the game.

▶ Can you learn the first part of the secret of the Fire Marble Domes and open the outer shell?

▶ Can you acquire the five-digit code that opens the inner lock and gives you access to a linking book?

▶ Have you learned how to read the D'ni symbols for the numerals 1 through 10? Having done that, can you figure out the pattern the numbers use in order to figure out the numerals 11 through 24? Finally, there is a chance that one symbol will represent the numeral 25. If that numeral occurs in the sequence, can you guess what it is?

▶ Have you associated a particular graphic symbol with each of the four domes?

▶ Have you learned what colors are represented by those symbols? Three of them are easy, but a fourth must be arrived at by guesswork.

▶ Have you reached the Map Room on Plateau Island, learned its secrets, and plotted the locations of five Fire Marble Domes on Riven?

▶ Have you deduced that the linking books in the Fire Marble Domes require power, figured out where that power must come from, and learned how to reach a final puzzle that will turn on that power?

▶ Have you solved the Marble Puzzle, which turns on the power to the linking books? You must correctly place five out of six colored marbles on a grid of 625 holes. You will only know three of the colors for certain; the fourth and fifth require a guesswork choice among the three remaining marbles.

If the correct marbles are in the proper holes when you pull the lever on the wall and then press a white button, an explosion of air around the marble device will tell you that the linking books are now powered and ready to use.

Once you reach Gehn's Age, what happens next depends on whether or not you have reached the Moiety Age and reacquired the Trap Book. You will have the opportunity to come and go among the five different islands of Riven. In addition, if you have not yet done so, you must solve the problem of reaching the Rebel Age to reacquire your stolen Trap Book. You may also visit Catherine on Prison Island, but each time you do so you will return to Gehn's Age until either you successfully trap him or he kills you.

After finishing Gehn's Age, you should have:

▶ Solved the Marble Puzzle that gives you access to Gehn's Age through any of the Fire Marble Domes.

▶ Found yourself in a prison cell in Gehn's home.

▶ Seen the five linking books arrayed about your prison cell, and recognized each as a link—initially unpowered—to one of the five islands of Riven.

▶ Found a button that calls Gehn into the room for a little chat.

▶ Listened to Gehn and either watched him turn on the power for all of the linking books or trapped him, escaped from the cage, and turned the power on for yourself.

- ▶ Used the Trap Book to capture Gehn and escape from your cell. This might be accomplished on a subsequent trip, rather than during the first visit to this Age.

- ▶ Used the linking book to the fifth island to visit Catherine, and seen the coded lock on her cell. This might be accomplished on this visit, or on a later one.

- ▶ Found the key (a series of specific sounds) somewhere in Gehn's residence that enables you to open Catherine's cell.

- ▶ Returned to Catherine's island and freed her.

Don't give up now! You're almost there!

WARNING! WHEN YOU SUMMON GEHN, HE TAKES THE TRAP BOOK FROM YOU AND THEN OFFERS YOU THE OPPORTUNITY OF GOING THROUGH AHEAD OF HIM. YOU MAY REFUSE. HE WILL ONLY GIVE YOU THREE CHANCES, HOWEVER, BEFORE HE DECIDES THAT YOU ARE NOT WORTH THE EFFORT, AND THEN HE KILLS YOU.

Puzzles and Problems on Catherine's Island

Although Gehn asks you not to, there is nothing stopping you from using the linking book outside your cell in his residence. Use it to journey to Prison Island where Catherine is being held prisoner. You can talk to Catherine, but you will not be able to free her from her prison cell unless you can crack the code to the three-keyed lock you encounter in the elevator.

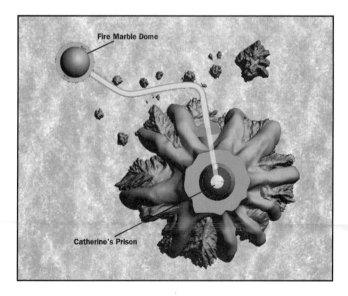

▶ Can you find the code to the lock somewhere in Gehn's residence? You can only do this if you've successfully trapped him in Atrus's Trap Book.

▶ Can you find the lever that opens your former cell? You need to open the cage in order to regain access to the five linking books.

When you leave Catherine's island for the last time, you should have:

▶ Freed Catherine from her cell.

▶ Received instructions from her regarding the telescope and the Star Fissure. You will need to solve one final puzzle before you successfully complete the game.

The Telescope Puzzle

You have one last puzzle to face now and, iron-ically, it's within a handful of steps from the very spot at which you first arrived on Riven. The telescope is the device that looks some-thing like a steel ice-cream cone suspended above a round hatch set into some iron plates on the ground. An eyepiece gives you a view of the hatch… or what's beyond it, presumably, if the hatch is open. A button raises or lowers the telescope for focus; a lever determines which way—up or down—the device moves.

Your goal is to open the hatch, and reveal a glass window looking into a field of stars with-in a deep fissure in the ground. Then use the tip of the telescope to break the glass and end the Riven Age.

▶ Have you figured out how to turn on the power to the telescope?

▶ Have you learned where the code to the hatch's locking device is kept, and used it to open the hatch?

▶ Have you found the locking pin that protects the glass from the telescope's descent?

▶ Have you smashed the glass?

 WARNING! DON'T OPERATE THE TELESCOPE UNTIL YOU'RE SURE YOU'RE READY TO END THE GAME! ONCE THE GLASS IS BROKEN, THERE'S NO TURNING BACK!

You have completed your final task when you have:

▶ Powered up the telescope.

▶ Unlocked the safety pin.

▶ Used the telescope to break the glass.

A few moments after Riven's final Armageddon has commenced, Atrus appears. What occurs next, and what he says, will depend on whether or not you have successfully done everything required of you, or whether some tasks remain unfinished when you finally open the Star Fissure.

You will have won the most complete victory possible if, when you open the Star Fissure, you have:

▶ Trapped Gehn.

▶ Freed Catherine.

If either or both of these tasks remain unfinished, you will be treated to a different ending, one less joyful than that resulting from complete success.

CHAPTER THREE
Puzzles and Problems: The Solutions

This is a wahrk chapter. It lists each of the major problems and puzzles of Riven and presents all of the solutions, with no attempt at concealing them. DON'T READ THIS CHAPTER, don't even page through it, if you want to have a chance of solving Riven's puzzles on your own!

The Gate Room

▶ The Gate Room is a five-sided chamber that rotates 72 degrees clockwise each time you press one of the rotation buttons at the outer doorways.

▶ The Gate Room has two open doorways. It rotates within a chamber that has five possible gateways. As the inner room turns, it opens connections between a different pair of gateways with each rotation.

▶ The geometry of the gate room looks like the following:

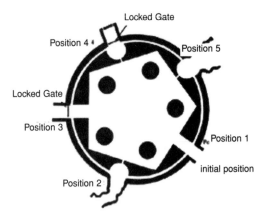

Locked Gate

Position 4

Position 5

Locked Gate

Position 3

Position 1

initial position

Position 2

▶ The five possible gateways are labeled 1 through 5. Position 1 is the first gate, on the southeast wall, which you encounter at the beginning of the game. The first time you enter the room, the open doors connect Positions 1 and 3.

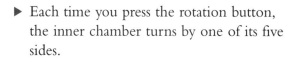
▶ Each time you press the rotation button, the inner chamber turns by one of its five sides.

▶ From Position 1, you can access Position 3. If you rotate the room three times, you can access Position 4.

▶ When you first encounter the Gate Room, lowered grates at Positions 3 and 4 block your access to the only two doors you can reach from Position 1. The switch to raise the grate at Position 4 is at Position 2, and the one to raise the position 3 grate is at Position 4. You need to access one of the other positions and go through in order to rotate the room again and gain access to the other gates.

▶ To do this, first press the rotation button at Position 1 four times to open the doorways at 5 and 2. (You are heading for Position 5, which is the one position that does not have a rotation button.) Then follow the outside path around and down to the wooden gate on the east side of the building. Click on the ground beneath the locked gate to crawl underneath and access the cave beyond. Go up through the cave to the open doorway. Go through to Position 2, where you will find the switch that raises the grate at Position 4, as well as the power valve for turning on the power to the telescope outside.

▶ From Position 2, rotate the inner room twice to align open doors at Positions 2 and 4. Go through to 4 where you will find the switch to raise the grate that blocks Position 3. A door locked from the other side prevents you from going to Position 4. Instead, from Position 4, rotate the room two more times to connect Positions 4 and 1. Go through to 1 and rotate twice. This opens the doors at 1 and 3, just as they were when you first entered this room. However, now the grate at 3 is raised, which enables you to continue your explorations in that direction.

The Magnetic Tram

▶ The trams on Riven are fairly straightforward and easy to figure out. A few points need to be kept in mind.

▶ The knob to the side of the main, central control rotates the car 180 degrees. Move it to the right or left to place the tram in position to go.

▶ The lever at the center makes the tram go. Once this switch is thrown, travel is automatic.

▶ Near each tram station is a silver sphere atop a stand or pedestal with a blue button or press-plate at the top. Press this to call a tram if none is waiting for you at the station.

▶ At Plateau Island, use the tram's rotation to allow you to turn in place, thereby reaching a door that is otherwise inaccessible.

The Submarine

▶ To lower the submarine into the water, follow the paths and piers counterclockwise around Village Lake on Jungle Island until you reach the Village. Continue to climb ladders and follow the one path you can until your reach the highest point beyond the Village, a ceremonial area where the submarine has been raised on a kind of elevator platform. Throw the lever to lower the sub into the water.

▶ Proceed back the way you came, down the ladders to the pier, and then clockwise around the lake, past the Jungle, past the clear-cut, past the rope bridge, down the stone steps past Sunner Rock, and then through a tunnel to emerge once again above the island's central lake. Go down the ladder beyond the Beetle Pool, and follow ladders and paths as far as you can go until you reach the ladder that leads into the submarine.

▶ Note that the submarine's stopping points are located in literal holes in the water. Some quirk of Gehn's technology or the physical laws of this universe enable water here to be shaped at will, creating holes and other peculiar, watery constructs. By studying the surface of the central lake from some elevated vantage point, you can deduce where the submarine stopping places are located.

▶ The submarine controls are simple. The rotating lever turns the sub around. The lever at the bottom can be moved left or right, and determines which fork in the tracks you will take when you move forward across a switch or track crossing. The lever to the right moves the sub forward to the next decision point.

▶ The submarine moves on wheels along an underwater track. The track configuration is as follows:

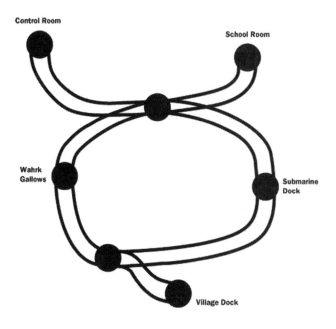

▶ To enter or leave the submarine, a ladder must be lowered from an access pier above the water. The first time you enter the sub, only the ladders at the sub dock and the control tower are lowered. You must go from the sub dock to the tower dock, leave the sub, and then climb a high ladder up the cliff to the control room in order to raise the levers that lower the other three ladders.

▶ With all the ladders down, you can access any of the five sites around the lake. From the sub dock and the village pier, you can leave the submarine and continue your travels elsewhere; the control tower and the school room, while important, are dead ends. Once you leave, you can only return to the sub.

▶ The Wahrk Gallows is a special case. The first time you leave the sub, you can walk around the open base of the gallows, but you will be unable to go anywhere else. Pulling the triangular handle on the chain lowers a bar on a rope, but you cannot reach it and after a moment or two, the rope automatically rises again. After finding your way to Gehn's Throne high above the Wahrk Gallows, you can close the base of the gallows, return to the gallows by submarine, lower the bar and ride it to the top, and find a ladder that you can lower to the lakeside walkway. When this task is complete, you can leave your sub at the gallows and continue your explorations elsewhere as well.

The Wahrk Idol

▶ At the end of a path in the jungle is a huge, brightly painted wooden construction that appears to be some kind of idol or religious totem designed to look like a wahrk. The path seems to end there.

▶ While standing between two posts or decorations with rounded tops, face the idol. Touch the top of the right-hand post. This raises a switch that opens the wahrk idol's mouth.

▶ Follow the stairs into the idol. A lever closes the mouth or opens it again. Beyond that point, an elevator can take you up to the jungle catwalks, Gehn's Throne, and the island's Fire Marble Dome, or down to the mag-tram that can transport you to Plateau Island.

▶ You can first penetrate the idol when you arrive from Plateau Island. When you emerge from the idol's mouth, you will see the raised switch on the post to your left. Clicking on the switch closes the idol's mouth once more.

The Wahrk Gallows

▶ To get to the Moiety Age, you must get past the Wahrk Gallows.

- ▶ Use the submarine to reach the Control Tower, which is one stop beyond the gallows (moving clockwise around the lake). In the Control Tower, raise all the levers to lower all of the ladders.

- ▶ When you learn the secret of the Wahrk Idol, follow the catwalk past the Jungle Island Fire Marble Dome and find the tower housing Gehn's Throne Room. Throw the left-hand lever to raise the Throne, and then throw the right-hand lever to close the base of the Wahrk Gallows, allowing access across the base.

- ▶ Use the submarine to reach the gallows and exit there. Cross to the center of the (now closed) base and pull the triangular handle on a chain.

- ▶ A bar hanging from a rope will lower. Grab the bar and ride it up to the top.

- ▶ From here, you can lower a ladder to the pier to ensure future access. You can also find the prison cell and its prisoner. From here, you can find your way through a secret passage to the Moiety Gateway Room.

D'ni Numbers

▶ Learn how to count in fluent D'ni by using the sub to reach the school room, which is one stop beyond the Control Tower. Play the wahrk counting game to learn the first 10 digits. Use the patterns you find here to deduce the numbers from 11 through 25.

▶ The D'ni use a base five counting system. In the base 10 system, which we use, we have distinct numerals for 1 through 9, with 10 represented as a 1 with a zero to the right of it to show a 1 in the tens' place. Count up another 10, and 20 is written as a 2 with a zero to the right to put it in the tens' place. In the D'ni system, they have unique symbols for 1 through 4; they then build on these through rotation and combination to create higher numerals.

▶ The D'ni numerals from 1 to 5 are:

| 1 | 2 | 3 | 4 | 5 |

Note that 5 is, in effect, a 1 rotated 90 degrees counterclockwise. (Yes, it could also have been rotated clockwise, but bear with us!)

▶ The numerals 6 through 9 are created by combining 5 plus one of the first 4 numerals. Thus, 9 is 5 + 4.

▶ The numeral 10 is a 2 rotated 90 degrees counterclockwise.

| 6 | 7 | 8 | 9 | 10 |

▶ The numerals 11 through 14 are comprised by combining 10 plus one of the first four numerals. Thus 12 is 10 + 2.

▶ The number 15 is made by rotating a 3 counterclockwise 90 degrees.

| 11 | 12 | 13 | 14 | 15 |

▶ The numerals 16 through 19 are made by combining 15 plus one of the first four numerals. Thus 18 is 15 + 3. Note that two of the lines in the figure are contiguous and look like a single line.

▶ The number 20 is a 4 rotated 90 degrees counterclockwise.

16   17   18   19   20

▶ The numerals 21 through 24 are made by combining 20 with one of the first four numerals: 21 is 20 + 1.

▶ The symbol for 25 is different.

21   22   23   24   25

▶ The first 25 D'ni numerals, then, are written as follows:

▶ A string of numbers, as for a five-digit code, would have the numerals written

side by side. For example, the code string
3 - 7 - 8 - 11 - 22 would be written:

| 3 | 7 | 8 | 11 | 22 |

▶ While exploring Riven, you should always be on the lookout for D'ni numerals. They always mean something important!

The Boiler

▶ The boiler is the first large structure you see on the beach when you arrive on Crater Island. It is used to boil wood chips (from logs transported from Jungle Island and reduced to splinters in the chipper) to create pulp for making paper, a vital component in Gehn's book-making experiments.

▶ You must solve the Boiler Puzzle to gain access to the boiler tank, cross a raised floor grating to a ladder leading down a drain in the center, and eventually reach the mountaintop. It's on this mountaintop where you can attempt to gain access to Gehn's laboratory.

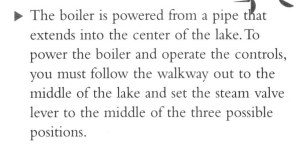

▶ The boiler is powered from a pipe that extends into the center of the lake. To power the boiler and operate the controls, you must follow the walkway out to the middle of the lake and set the steam valve lever to the middle of the three possible positions.

▶ You must set the boiler controls a certain way in order to gain access to the tank's interior and the ladder in the center.

▶ The first control is on the left of the walkway around the boiler building as you approach the main controls; a valve lever can be set to one of two positions. The higher/farther position powers the water pumps for filling and emptying the boiler. The lower/nearer position powers the grating.

- ▶ The main controls consist of a wheel to the left which fills or drains the tank, a lever to the right which turns the furnace on or off, and a switch at the upper right that raises or lowers a grate inside the tank.

- ▶ To enter the boiler, the furnace must be turned off. When it's on, you will hear a roar, a red light is visible by the boiler door, and the door itself is locked.

- ▶ To enter, the tank must be empty. Make sure the power at the "Y junction" is switched to the far/high pipe. Turn the large wheel to move the pipe and watch the water drain away through the vertical glass view port.

- ▶ To enter the boiler and get across to the ladder, the floor grating must be raised. Make sure the valve at the "Y junction" is set to the nearer/lower branch. Throw the switch at the upper right, and watch the grate rise into position. If the grate was up and you've just lowered it, throw the switch again to reposition it.

- ▶ With the furnace off, the tank empty, and the grate raised, you can enter the boiler tank and reach the ladder.

Gehn's Laboratory

▶ To reach Gehn's laboratory on Crater Island, you must go through the following steps.

▶ Go through the drain pipe after solving the Boiler Puzzle (see previous section). Emerge on the mountain and follow a path across the rocks and down onto a railed platform on the cliff face.

▶ Open the round hatch, which was locked from underneath. This gives you access to the beach and the boiler again, should you need it.

▶ Go through the double doors and then close them to reveal hidden passageways to left and right.

▶ Follow the right-hand passage as you face the doors from the inside. Find a lever against the rocks and pull it, which turns off the ventilation fans inside. (This walkway also leads to the front of Gehn's lab, which is locked, and then to the West Drawbridge and the Great Golden Dome.)

▶ Return to the double doors and turn left. Follow the steps down to the frog-catching chamber.

▶ With the ventilator fans off, you can click on the grating above the frog trap apparatus to open the shaft and crawl inside.

▶ Follow the ventilator shaft until you come to another opening. Click on the grate to open it and drop into Gehn's lab.

▶ You can now unlock the front door, read Gehn's lab journal, and use the tram out the back door to travel to Plateau Island.

▶ Make sure you read the lab journal and take note of the numerical code inside. You can't take the journal with you.

The Map Table Puzzle

▶ On Plateau Island, you will find a rather fiendish puzzle—it's easy to work, but difficult to interpret. You must solve this puzzle, however, to complete the Marble Puzzle you encounter later.

▶ When you ride the elevator up to the mountaintop, you will have access to two areas: A spot overlooking five plateaus, which represent the five islands of Riven; and a large, circular building, the Map Room, in the center of a lake. The two sites are connected by a path that runs through the elevator and across a narrow walkway that may extend into the lake.

▶ At the overlook, look down to see the control panel, a plate with five buttons, each shaped like the graphic designs representing the five different islands. Push one of the buttons; note how the plateau below the overlook representing that island changes (water flows onto the top, assuming the shape of that island's mountainous terrain). (Water on Riven, as you may have noticed by now, does not behave the same way that it does in more mundane universes!)

▶ Cross the path from the overlook to the Map Room. The walkway now extends out to the Map Room.

▶ The Map Table is a large grid divided into a five-by-five array of large squares, 25 squares in all.

▶ One square on the Map Table represents one square in the small island symbol below.

▶ Elsewhere in your travels (on a plaque inside the entrance to the Great Golden Dome, on the mosaic behind one of the beetles in the Gate Room, and on the control panel at the overlook on Plateau Island), you have seen small graphic designs representing the five islands of Riven. You will see them again on the linking books to each of the islands. The array before you—the Map Table—represents the same shapes.

▶ When you press one of the island-shaped buttons at the overlook above the plateaus, that island shows the shape of its terrain with oddly flowing water. At the same time, that particular island is displayed here, in the Map Room.

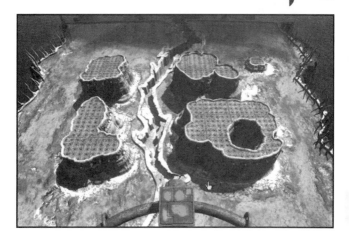

▶ One of the large squares of the island display will be highlighted in yellow. Press that square, or any other, to access a holographic image of the terrain in that square. Note the blue lines further dividing the terrain into a five-by-five grid of small squares.

▶ You must conclude that the puzzle requires you to note the locations of each of the Fire Marble Domes on the five islands of Riven, one dome for each island. You should be able to make this deduction when you see the Marble Puzzle in the upper level of the Golden Dome, after you see the 25x25 grid and the six colored marbles to the right. (You will only need five of the six marbles, a further twist to this admittedly fiendish puzzle.)

▶ To solve the Map Table Puzzle on Plateau Island, carefully examine each square, and search for identifying terrain features that will enable you to locate the dome locations.

▶ To record your deductions, you must work out some sort of coordinate system. For the purposes of this guide book, we number each of the large squares of each island, starting from the upper left, going left to right and top to bottom.

▶ Next, in each large square, the small squares are identified by labeling the columns across A, B, C, D, and E, and numbering the rows down 1, 2, 3, 4, and 5.

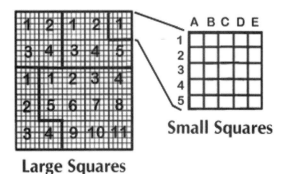

Large Squares

Small Squares

▶ Examine each map carefully, using the handle beneath the map to rotate the map. You are looking for a flat square where the dome could reside. In some cases, there are identifiable terrain features to guide you.

▶ The Fire Marble Dome on Crater Island (in the upper-left corner) is directly beneath a crater or hole in a mountaintop.

▶ The dome on Plateau Island is just behind a narrow, V-shaped cleft in the rock wall of the central lake.

▶ The dome on Temple Island is on a flat piece of land that extends beyond the circle of the Great Dome.

▶ The dome on Jungle Island is located on a cylindrical pillar of stone.

▶ Prison Island's dome is on a spit of land that extends out into the sea at the southeastern edge.

▶ The exact positions can be plotted as follow:

ISLAND	LARGE SQUARE	SMALL SQUARE
Crater Island	1	B4
Plateau Island	4	A2
Temple Island	2	A1
Jungle Island	5	D2
Prison Island	1	B1

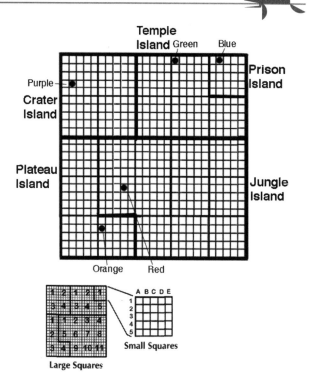

The Moiety Age

▶ You must reach the Moiety Age at some point in your quest in order to recover your Trap Book and to find Catherine's journal.

▶ To open the gateway to the Moiety Age, you must acquire some clues from Jungle Island (plus one missing piece from Plateau Island).

▶ Find the silhouette of a frog near the tram that brings you to Jungle Island. The wooden eye has the D'ni numeral "3" on the back and makes a song like a frog's chirp.

▶ Find the silhouette of a beetle in a stone pool you fill with water on the way to the access ladder at the submarine pen. The wooden eye had the numeral "2" on the back and makes a sound like the whirr-click of a beetle.

▶ Find the silhouette of a wahrk in the rocks on the lagoon past Sunner Rock. The wooden eye has the D'ni numeral "5" and makes a whale-like sound similar to a wahrk. You can confirm this by calling a wahrk and hearing its cry when you are in Gehn's underwater Viewing Chamber on Plateau Island. The wahrk approaches your vantage point if you use the Color Wheel to turn on the red light outside.

▶ Find the fourth eye in the jungle, off the path just below the spot where a large dagger is thrust point-down into the earth. There is no animal silhouette here, but the eye makes the distinctive bark of a sunner, which you have heard if you were able to sneak close to the sunners on their basking rock earlier.

▶ Find the fifth silhouette (that of a fish with a vaguely delta-form shape) in the viewer on Plateau Island in Gehn's underwater Viewing Chamber. Although you may think you see the wooden eye through the viewer, you cannot reach the spot. You must deduce that the number associated with the fish is "1."

▶ When you reach the Moiety Gateway, a room with a circle of 25 stones, each with the graphic image of a different Rivenese life form, you must touch the five stones in the correct sequence.

▶ The images and the sequence are:

Fish	Beetle	Frog	Sunner	Wahrk

▶ If you click on the wrong stone or in the wrong order, nothing will happen. You must touch the stones already moved in reverse order to back out of the mistake, and then begin again with the correct sequence. The stones will automatically reset when a sixth stone is pressed.

The Fire Marble Domes (First Step)

▶ At some point, you must enter a different age or world, the place Gehn calls his residence, a universe he calls "233." (Gehn has been working on a lot of universes! Riven is his fifth!)

▶ You can reach Gehn's world by using the linking book inside any of the Fire Marble Domes you see during your explorations.

▶ To open a rotating Fire Marble Dome, you must approach one of the kinetoscopes facing the dome and look through the eyepiece.

▶ As you look through the eyepiece, the rotating shutter creates a kind of animation, enabling you to see the changing symbols on the rotating dome blend into a kind of movie. One of the symbols, however, is marked in yellow; you will see it flash this color as it goes past.

▶ Click the button on top of the kinetoscope to catch the yellow symbol as it appears. This will take some practice and several tries, but keep at it. When you click on the correct symbol, both the rotating shutter and the dome stop spinning. The dome will then open, and for just an instant, you will see the linking book inside. Then an inner dome will lock shut, a second puzzle that you must solve in order to link with Gehn's world.

▶ Sketch or otherwise note the symbol that opens each dome, and remember which island you found it on. The symbols refer to specific colors; you must know what color goes with which island in order to solve the Marble Puzzle later on.

▶ The kinetoscope for the Fire Marble Dome on Plateau Island is broken. You can stop that dome by simply clicking on the switch rapidly—basically, just click the mouse as fast as you can—and catching the appropriate symbol randomly. This method, incidentally, can be used on any of the domes, should you have trouble catching the correct symbol as it flashes past. When you hit it, you will hear a change in the sound made by the rotating shutter, and the device will spin down. A moment later, the dome will open.

▶ Because the kinetoscope is broken, you must determine the correct symbol for the Plateau Island by careful observation of the dome while it is still spinning.

The Fire Marble Domes (Second Step)

▶ To reach the linking book inside a Fire Marble Dome, you must get the correct five-digit code and use it to position the sliders along the scale on the inner dome lock. When the sliders are correctly positioned, push the button. The sliders will move all the way to the left and the dome will open. If the setting is wrong, the sliders move to the left, but nothing else happens. You can then try again.

▶ The code is located in Gehn's lab journal in his laboratory on Crater Island. The code is different each time you play Riven.

- ▶ The code is a string of five D'ni numerals, but some will be higher than 10. Because the wahrk-gallows toy in the school room only teaches you the numerals through 10, you must figure out how the numbering system works in order to translate higher numbers.

  If you have trouble, consult the section earlier in this chapter on D'ni numerals.

- ▶ After entering the correct combination and pushing the button, the inner shield raises and you can access the book. The book will not transport you to Gehn's world, however, unless you have also solved the Marble Puzzle, described earlier in this chapter, and provided the books with power.

▶ The scale on the lock has 25 positions, marked off by fives. Move the right-most slider to the point on the scale corresponding to the highest, right-most number of the code. Move the next slider in line to the next highest number, the second from the right. Continue down the list of numbers, until the last, left-most slider is placed on the last, left-most number in the line.

▶ When you use the Linking Book inside the dome, you will arrive in Gehn's residence in Age 233 (or in D'ni notation, 98). When you use a Linking Book from this location to a specific island, you will arrive inside the Fire Marble Dome of that island. To exit the dome, move back from the book and click on the button you see on the floor to the right of the book. The dome will open and you can step out.

The Marble Puzzle

▶ The solution to the Marble Puzzle requires that you solve the Map Table Puzzle on Plateau Island, described earlier in this chapter.

▶ Each of the symbols associated with a different Fire Marble Dome (the symbols used to open the dome with its kinetoscope) represents a color. The colors and symbols, with their respective islands, are as follows:

COLOR	ISLAND
Green	Temple Island
Red	Jungle Island
Purple	Crater Island
Orange	Plateau Island
Blue	Prison Island
Yellow	None

Note that you must guess at the color for the Prison Island, because you won't be able to reach that Fire Marble Dome until after you have solved the Marble Puzzle. Note, too, that you must guess at the color associated with the Crater Island symbol, because that light (violet) is broken on the Color Wheel.

▶ The Marble Puzzle array, which is obviously based on the map array on Plateau Island, must be mentally divided into the graphic logos for the five islands.

▶ Each large island square is numbered, running left to right, top to bottom.

▶ Each large island square is further divided into a five-by-five grid. For simplicity, mentally label the vertical columns of each A, B, C, D, and E, going left to right, and the horizontal rows 1, 2, 3, 4, and 5, going top to bottom.

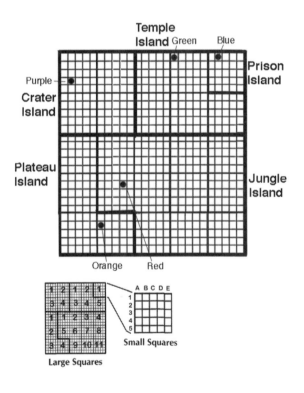

▶ The proper marble placement for each island is as follows:

ISLAND	COLOR	LARGE SQUARE	COORDINATES
Crater Island	Purple	1	B4
Temple Island	Green	2	A1
Prison Island	Blue	1	B1
Plateau Island	Orange	4	A2
Jungle Island	Red	5	D2

▶ When the marbles are properly placed, move the lever on the wall, and then press the white button. An explosion of air from beneath the marble press signals that power has been provided to the linking books.

Trapping Gehn

▶ You need the Trap Book Atrus gave you to capture Gehn. It was taken from you when you first arrived in Riven. To get it back, you must solve the puzzle of the Moiety Gateway, enter the Rebel Age, and get the trap book from Nelah, one of Catherine's allies.

▶ While you are behind bars in Gehn's residence, Gehn will take the book, which he thinks is a gateway to the world of D'ni. After considering going through, he reconsiders and asks you to go through first.

▶ Although at first glance this seems to be suicide, it is in fact what you must do. Touch the image on the book, and you will find yourself trapped inside. You will see Gehn looking at you, but he is in fact seeing a moving image of the subterranean world of D'ni. After a moment, he will touch the image and follow you in.

▶ If you played Myst, you already know how Trap Books work. When Gehn touches the image, he trades places with you. He is now inside the book, while you are in his home, free to explore outside the bars of your cage.

WARNING! DON'T TOUCH THE IMAGE IN THE BOOK AGAIN, OR YOU WILL ONCE AGAIN TRADE PLACES WITH GEHN—THIS TIME PERMANENTLY!

Releasing Catherine

▶ You can reach Catherine's island only through the linking book in Gehn's residence. First, either Gehn must turn the power on to all of the books before you trap him, or you must turn the power on after you trap him.

▶ Trap Gehn by entering the Trap Book yourself. When he follows, you exchange places with him, trapping him in the book and leaving you outside the cage.

▶ Go to the ladder leading down to Gehn's bed chamber. Go to his bedside table and open the gray sphere, which is a kind of timepiece. As it opens, note the progression of clinking sounds.

▶ Return upstairs and find the lever that lowers the cage around the Linking Book's access.

▶ Go to Catherine's island using the Linking Book with the single square. Enter the same sequence of sounds you heard from Gehn's watch using the three keys in the elevator, and then pull the lever.

▶ The bars will open, the elevator will rise, and Catherine, freed at last, will join you.

The Telescope

▶ Get the code of five D'ni numbers from Catherine's journal.

▶ Make sure the valve located in the cavern at Position 2 is turned to point to the right, providing power to the telescope assembly.

▶ Enter the numbers to open the hatch on the steel plates beneath the telescope.

▶ Move the pin on the support strut at the left to enable the telescope to go down.

▶ Lower the lever, then press and hold the green button to move the telescope down until the glass is cracked and the Star Fissure is opened.

Things Not To Do In Riven

Although Riven is not a violent or combat-oriented game, there are a few things that you should avoid if at all possible. In some cases, you can even get killed.

▶ Do not use the trap book yourself when Gehn is not around. You will be trapped there forever, and Atrus will be very upset.

▶ When Gehn offers you a chance to touch the trap book image, do not continue to refuse him. After three refusals, he will stop wasting time on you, and kill you. Well, what did you expect of someone who smokes frogs and plays God with people's lives?

▶ When you trap Gehn, do not touch the image of D'ni again! You will exchange places with him once more, and this time, become trapped forever.

▶ Do not power up and operate the telescope before you have trapped Gehn. If you do, Atrus will appear and, moments later, so will Gehn, along with one of his guards. Gehn will kill both Atrus and you.

▶ Do not operate the telescope before you rescue Catherine. If you capture Gehn but do not free Catherine, you have won a limited and melancholy victory at best. In this scenario, you and Atrus have survived, but Atrus may never see his wife again, and the Rivenese themselves may all die in a world's collapse. Pity Atrus! He has lost his beloved Catherine, the world he has labored to save, and his father, all at the same time!

CHAPTER FOUR
Walkthrough: All Revealed

This is a wahrk chapter. Don't read it, don't even skim through it, unless you want a lot of the fun and mystery of Riven spoiled for you!

This chapter gives away *everything*, without worrying about how or where you get much of the information, and with scarcely a nod toward the rich and atmospheric wonder that is the world of Riven. Follow this outline if you want to get from beginning to end in the shortest and most direct possible time.

A *much* better idea is to play the game and figure out the puzzles for yourself, or at most, with a little help from other chapters in this book! Then look here and compare with this walkthrough how well you did and to see what *other* endings you might have encountered!

Also, with a game like Riven, there is no one right or best way to travel through the various locations or to gather the necessary clues. The order of events in this walkthrough is significantly—and deliberately—different from the order set in Chapter 5, "Walking Through Riven." In most cases, what is important is that you assemble the clues and solve the puzzles, not the order in which you do so.

With that said, let's begin!

The Walkthrough

Temple Island: The Gate Room

▶ When you are released from the cage, check out the mechanism ahead. It's a telescope, but it seems to be pointed at a sealed hatch on a portion of the ground covered by iron plates. Note the lever to the right with a button in the middle— neither works. The mechanism has no power.

▶ Go back toward the cage you arrived in, go to the left, and follow the steps up.

Briefly venture out onto the bridge that leads to your right, stop, turn, and look back to see the enormous golden dome behind and to the left of the Gate Room. This is your first goal.

▶ Return back the way you came on the bridge and continue straight into the Gate Room antechamber. Note a button on the wall to your right, and the open door ahead that leads into the Gate Room. Proceed into the Gate Room.

▶ Explore the Gate Room. It is five-sided with two open doors, currently at Positions 1 (where you came in) and 3, which is blocked by a grating. You must open the grating to go through the second doorway at 3, which leads to the giant golden dome. Note the beetles on the pillars. The pull ring at the tail of each beetle reveals a small painting, different for each. A *very* close look at each of the three walls covered with indecipherable writing reveals tiny pinholes through the stone.

▶ To use the Gate Room, you must understand its geometry. There are five possible gateways, numbered for easy discussion, starting at 1 (on the southeast wall, where you entered), and proceeding clockwise around the room, 2, 3, 4, and 5. Pushing any of the rotation buttons outside the Gate Room rotates the room by one wall: 72 degrees.

▶ Return to the antechamber. You begin with open gates aligned at 1 and 3. Push the button on the right to rotate the Gate Room clockwise 72 degrees. At this point, the gate into the room is closed, but you can peek through a small lens in the recess in front of you and see the room's interior.

▶ The room's open gates are now aligned with Positions 2 and 4. Push the rotation button again to turn the gateways to Positions 3 and 5. Push it again to turn the gates to Positions 4 and 1. The gateway in front of you is now open once again. Note that the gate at Position 4 is closed off by a grate.

▶ Push the button to rotate the room one more time. The open gateways should now be at 2 and 5. Return to the path, turn left, and follow the steps down. When you've gone as far as you can, turn left twice to face a locked gate. Click under the gate to go inside. Go up the ladder and across a board. Ahead, note the open door into the Gate Room at Position 5.

▶ Go through the Gate Room and into the cave at Position 2. Throw the steam-valve lever, which turns on the power to the telescope apparatus outside. (You won't need this until the end of the game, but you might as well take care of this little chore now.) Turn around and head back toward the Gate Room. Note the rotation button to the right of the door, and a lever to the left. Throw the lever to raise the grate that closes off Position 4.

▶ Push the rotation button twice to open Positions 2 and 4. Go through the Gate Room to Position 4. The grating is raised now, enabling access to an antechamber at 4, but the way beyond is blocked by a massive door. Obviously, you'll need to go somewhere else to open this door. Turn around to see another handle on the left side of the door. Throw it to lower the grate you originally noticed at Position 3.

▶ Push the rotate button twice to move the openings to Positions 4 and 1. Go across the Gate Room to the main entrance and rotate twice to align Positions 1 and 3. With the grate at Position 3 now raised, cross the room to Position 3.

▶ Go across the bridge to the Great Golden Dome. Note the lever in the dome doorway. Operating the lever does nothing; you will need to restore power. Put the lever back to the position in which you found it.

▶ Enter the giant chamber. Note the sign, which shows island symbols and indicates that this chamber connects with all five. It also shows the catwalk you are standing on, with a missing piece at 5 o'clock. If you look to your right, you can see the missing catwalk section, and what looks like a large wheel on the far side.

▶ Follow the catwalk to the left, and follow a long flight of stairs as you circle halfway around the chamber. Outside, there's a short catwalk extending out from the main walkway, where a vertical pipe is bleeding off steam. Throw the steam valve lever to turn power on to the West Drawbridge (which connects the Golden Dome with Crater Island). Return to the main catwalk and follow it to the left. Note the elevator button on the rock face as you pass, but continue around the outside of the giant dome, passing into and through a rock tunnel. Exit the tunnel and you'll find another steam valve. Throw the lever to restore power to the bridge that connects the giant dome with the Gate Room.

▶ Turn around and head back through the tunnel. As you emerge from the tunnel, notice the button set in the wall to your left. At the moment, it's not operational, but remember it. You may need it later.

▶ Now return to the Golden Dome and go through it up the stairs. At the entrance, throw the lever and watch the bridge raise and extend to a position somewhere above you. Lower the bridge again and return to the Gate Room. Go through to Position 1. You have now solved the Gate Room puzzle.

Temple Island: The Temple

▶ Cross the bridge to the temple area of the island. Go through the entrance and down a passageway. Go to the door on the left of the passageway and enter the Temple Imaging Room. Note the throne in the chamber. The button on the right as you sit in the throne lowers and raises a cage structure over you. The lever on the left probably controls imaging.

▶ From here you can see two small imaging devices. Go to the device to the left of the door and throw the lever up to open a door in a room filled with pillars (the Temple downstairs). Return to the passageway. Go left and down, entering the Temple by opening a heavy stone door.

▶ Note the throne display set between statues of giant fish-creatures (wahrks) with offerings. Obviously, someone sitting in the throne in the smaller room upstairs can have his image projected into this caged-in throne area in the temple, an effect that might make him seem godlike in his power.

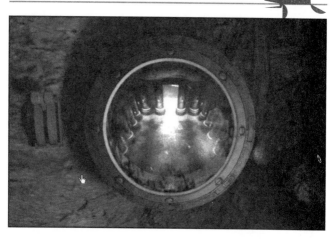

▶ Turn around to see the open temple door, just to the left of the hidden door behind the pillars through which you entered the room. Go through the open door and go right to a mag-lev tramline. Note the blue-lit sphere next to the steps. Press the top to call a tram car to the station.

▶ Get into the tram. Throw the knob to the left around to the right to rotate the car. Then push the power lever forward to go. You're about to start a wild ride to Jungle Island.

Jungle Island: From the Sunners to the Submarine

▶ When you leave the car, turn to your right. Move forward, and then turn right again. Look until you find a small wooden device painted like a crude eye. Rotate the eye and carefully note the symbol carved on the back. Also, listen to the *creak-chirp* sound the eye makes as it turns. Finally, turn around and go up the stairs directly ahead of you. At the landing, turn around and look back the way you came. Do you see the outline of the tunnel mouth? It's shaped somewhat like a frog with the wooden Eye appearing in the same relative position as the eye of a real frog.

▶ Follow the steps up. Note the blue light sphere—yet another tram call button. Go out of the tunnel and down the stone steps. At the cross path, turn left and keep going down.

▶ Ahead, note some animals sunning on a rock just below the path. As you approach, they raise their heads and make deep, "whuffling" noises. Wait until their heads are down and they stop moving, then approach another step, leaving the path and moving slowly down onto the beach. If you move too quickly (clicking to move when their heads are up), you will scare them off.

▶ If you move cautiously enough, you will reach the beach, where one of the sunners will raise its head and deliver a loud, distinctive bark. Note the sound. You'll need to recall it later.

▶ As long as you're down here, turn right, and then follow the beach around the sunners' lagoon to the left. Note the steps in the distance, but follow the beach to the left as far as you can. Turn around and look at the rocks which form the rough shape of the fish-creature (a wahrk) that you saw in the temple and another wooden Eye.

▶ Move onto the sandbar to reach the Eye. Move it to see another symbol and hear a sound resembling a whale's call. Note the symbol and the sound—both are important.

▶ Return to the beach where you saw the sunners. Go back up the rocks to the path and turn left. Follow the path up the steps you saw from the beach and enter the tunnel. Emerge on a rickety, wooden walkway and follow it to the end. Up ahead you can see a guard tower, where a guard is sounding the alarm.

▶ From here you can look out across an inner lagoon, a lake filling a huge, circular crater. Note a peculiar spherical vehicle on a high ledge to the left. Beyond, you can see a number of strange, spherical buildings.

▶ Go down the ladder and note the dry pool. Turn the petcock on the right to fill the pool. Note the beetle shape formed by the water along with another wooden Eye. Turn the Eye to note both the symbol and a *whirr-click* sound. You'll need to remember them.

▶ Go around Beetle Pool and down the ladder. Follow the walkway to the left. Note what look like holes in the water of Village Lake, and various curious structures around the crater's inner walls. Go into a short tunnel. Find a ladder that leads down into a hole in the water. You can't go any farther from here.

▶ Go back up the ladders, along the walkway, and past the beach all the way to the T-intersection landing. Go past the landing where you came in, and go up the steps in front of you. At the top, cross a rope-and-plank bridge. Note the clear-cut area and jungle beyond with gate and paths. Follow the path to the right when it branches, take the next left, and then turn toward a gate. Note a beetle crawling on the gate post. Click on it to hear the sound it makes, a kind of *whirr-click* you heard previously when you turned the wooden Eye at the beetle-shaped pool. Go through the gate into the forest.

▶ Follow the path. Go down the steps and note the volcanic rumbling in the distance. Go through a tree, past luminous fungus.

▶ Turn around and look for a giant dagger. Turn right at the dagger, follow the steps down, and click on the light. Here's yet another wooden Eye.

▶ Turn the Eye and hear a sunner bark. Note the symbol—there is no animal silhouette associated with this Eye.

▶ Return to the main path and proceed left. See the red glow and hear the rumble again. Take the left-hand path at the Y intersection. Go through the gate, turn left, and up the steps to find yourself back in the clear-cut on what had been the left path when you first approached this area. Go back to the gate. Note the turning fire marble. Go back to the Y intersection. Take the left path (the right path when you first approached this Y intersection). Go along the walkway and down.

▶ Ahead, you can see a giant wahrk idol at the end of the path. There is a cunningly hidden switch on top of the post to the right. Click here to raise the switch and open the wahrk idol's mouth, revealing steps that lead up.

▶ Follow the steps and note the tram call and a wooden elevator. Turn around to find the lever that closes the wahrk idol's mouth. Turn back and enter the elevator. Go down, turn around, and go through to another tramcar station. Return to the elevator and go up two levels, above the level where you entered the idol's mouth.

▶ Emerge from the elevator on a catwalk high above the forest floor. Follow the walkway around to the right. Go past a branching to the right to reach a rotating Fire Marble Dome.

▶ Examine the dome carefully. You'll see these things on every island you visit. Note the symbols flickering past on the rotating dome, and note that one seems to be marked in yellow.

▶ Go back to the branch you passed earlier and follow it to a device facing the dome called a kinetoscope. Watch the changing symbols through the eyepiece; click the button on top when the yellow symbol appears in the viewer. (**NOTE:** If you have trouble catching it at just the right moment, rapidly click the mouse button. Sooner or later, you'll get it.) The device will stop rotating, as will the large dome. Note the symbol that opened the dome; you'll need to recognize it later.

▶ Go to the now open Fire Marble Dome. Look through the circular window and note what looks like a book inside. Move the sliders and press the button. Nothing happens; obviously, you need to learn a code to open the dome further.

▶ Turn around and exit the dome, turning left to climb a flight of steps to a tower. Open the door and go inside. Note the wahrk skull chair.

▶ When you are seated in the throne, the left handle raises and turns the throne, moving it up to a position from which you can look down on Village Lake. Almost directly below is a circular platform beneath a high tower—it's the Wahrk Gallows, a place of bloody execution.

▶ Turn the right handle to close the bottom platform on the gallows. Note the tracks underneath the water in the lake.

▶ Move the left handle to go back down and leave the room. Go out and back along the walkways to the elevator. Go down one level to the wahrk idol. Open the lever and exit.

▶ Go along the path, toward the tunnel beneath the marble dome, and emerge to see a native child run away from you. Go to the Y intersection and take the right path. Go up the steps and through the gate. Turn right on the catwalk.

▶ Follow the catwalk around to the inside wall of Village Lake. Note a small island above the surface with something that might be a telescope or imaging lens on it. Approach the village of dried mud spheres. Climb the ladders and cross a narrow plank to a house. (If you like, click on the star-shaped doorknocker, and get a glimpse of someone who obviously doesn't want to talk to strangers.)

▶ Follow the walkway to the left, going up a ladder and along the catwalk. Approach a spherical, mechanical contraption, otherwise known as the submarine. Throw the lever on the left to lower the sub into the water. Note the ceremonial area, where large creatures (wahrks, perhaps?) are cut up and their flesh hung up to dry.

▶ Return along the walkways and ladders. In front of the house with the plank, look into the lagoon and see the sub now resting in a hole in the water on the underwater tracks.

▶ Follow the walkway back around the lake, past the gate to the Fire Marble Dome, and up and out past the clear-cut. Cross the rope bridge, go back down past the now-empty Sunner Rock, and follow the paths and ladders past the Beetle Pool and down to the last ladder, which now gives you access to the lowered submarine. You're now ready for a drive around the bottom of Village Lake.

Jungle Island: The Submarine Circuit

▶ Determine how the controls work. The turning handle at the center makes the sub change direction; the lever at the bottom determines which track (left or right) the sub will take at the next track junction;

the lever to the right moves the vehicle forward to the next siding or decision point. The gauge at the top right shows when the sub is powered and ready to move.

▶ Turn the sub around, and then move forward twice. Look up, open the hatch, and climb the ladder to the Ladder Control Room.

▶ You will find three lever handles that are down, two that are up. Throw the three handles so that all are up. This extends all submarine access ladder bridges around the lake.

▶ Return to the sub and turn it around. Go forward onto the main track, and then left at the next siding. Exit the sub and follow the path into the village school room.

▶ There are several things of interest here, including a cage with a turn-crank that projects a 3-D holograph of Gehn. Turn the crank and get a feel for his evident enjoyment in playing God.

▶ Go to the wahrk hangman game. Moving the ring at the base accesses a random symbol and lowers one of the two hanging figures a random distance toward the waiting wahrk at the bottom.

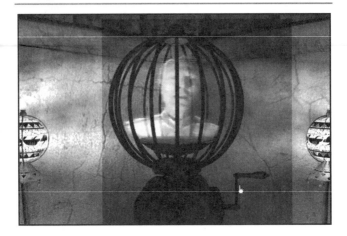

▶ The symbols, you now realize, are numbers. You can learn what symbol represents which number by counting the clicks with each turn. Play the game until you have learned all of the D'ni numbers from 1 to 10.

▶ What do you think of a world where the children play games that randomly sacrifice victims to hungry monsters? Remember, Gehn *rules* this world!

▶ You now know that the symbols you've been finding behind the wooden Eyes are numbers. The Eye at the frog shape near the tram station was numbered 3. The Eye on the stones that looked like a wahrk was numbered 5. The Eye in the jungle that played the sunner bark was numbered 4. The Eye in the Beetle Pool was numbered 2. This gives you a useful series: Beetle = 2. Frog = 3. Sunner = 4. Wahrk = 5. You don't know what animal is number 1, nor do you know yet what the sequence signifies.

▶ Return to the sub. Reverse its direction and go forward one. Make sure the left track is selected, and then go forward once more. Exit the sub at the Wahrk Gallows.

▶ Cross to the center of the gallows. Pull the triangular hanging handle to lower a bar. Click on the bar to carry yourself up to the top of the gallows. Pass between the wahrk skulls toward a barred, circular portal. Look inside to see a native being held captive.

Jungle Island: Find the Gateway
to the Moiety Age

▶ Turn right and follow the walkway to a
star-shaped control in the rock. Activate
the control and watch the portal open.
The native is gone, vanished, it seems, into
thin air.

▶ Click on the drainage grate on the floor.
Click on the dirty water beneath the grating to open a secret panel in the back wall
of the cell. Go through the opening.

▶ Go into the tunnel and hear the door
close behind you. Seven clicks in the darkness takes you to a light.

▶ Click on the branch on the left to turn on
a light. Turn around and go up to where
you can just see another light. Touch the

bulb to turn it on and extend the light further. Move ahead one and touch another
light. Move ahead one more to see a door.
Move ahead one more and touch the light,
then turn to see the door on the right.
Opening the door to the right closes the
door to the left. Follow the new passage.

▶ Enter a circle of 25 stone pillars decorated
with graphic animal totems. At this point,
you do not have enough information to
solve the totem puzzle. The sequence
Beetle = 2, Frog = 3, Sunner = 4, and
Wahrk = 5 may apply here, but you still
don't know what the first symbol is. You
could try solving it by brute force, trying
one animal followed by the four you know
in sequence and then resetting the whole
thing and starting all over with another animal as 1, and another, and another… There
is a better way, however; leave it for now.

▶ Return up the passage and head toward the secret door in the prison cell. Pull the handle on the ground to the right to open the secret door. Return through the empty prison cell.

▶ Go right out of the prison door and follow the catwalk. Click on the ladder to lower it to the lower level of the catwalk. Climb down the ladder, turn around, and follow the catwalk back clockwise around the lagoon.

▶ Continue along the path and out the gate into the clear-cut area. Take a left, followed by a right to a square tunnel, and go down the tunnel to the logging car ride. Pull the handle on the left to start the car.

Crater Island

▶ Arrive at Crater Island and get dumped into a log chipper. Go down the ladder and find the boiler in the distance. Check the ladder behind the chipper on the rock. It leads to a round hatch, which in turn leads to the logging car for a return trip to Jungle Island.

▶ Go past the boiler to the right and follow the beach around the lake counterclockwise to find a very tall, narrow ladder. The ladder leads to a hatchway that's up the side of the cliff. The hatch is locked from this side, so you can't get through. Note the building farther down the cliff. This is Gehn's laboratory, your eventual goal.

▶ Go to the long, narrow pier that extends into the middle of the lake. There you will find a valve handle with three possible positions. Turning it to the position farthest to the left powers the log chipper. Turning it to the middle position powers the boiler. Turning it to the right (the position in which you find it) powers the frog-catching apparatus in a cave near Gehn's laboratory. Set the valve to the middle position.

▶ Return to the boiler and check it out. The door won't open, and there's a red light on outside the door.

▶ Go back around the outside catwalk to the right to find the boiler controls. The first lever at the Y junction controls the routing of power from the pipe leading out to the middle of the lake. The upper (left fork of the Y) lever powers the pumps that fill or drain the boiler. The lower (right fork of the Y) lever powers a grate that can move up or down inside the boiler. Leave the lever on the upper (left) setting.

▶ Turn to the right and examine the boiler controls. The lever at the lower right controls the heat for the boiler. You can hear a roar, as from a furnace. Turn this lever to the upright position and note that the roar stops and the water in the tank stops boiling.

▶ The wheel at the left moves a pipe that enables you to fill or empty the tank with water. Turn the wheel and watch the water level in the tank fall.

▶ A switch to the upper right controls the position of the movable floor grate inside the tank. First, turn to your left and switch the power valve from the upper (left fork) position to the lower (right fork) position. Then face the main controls again and raise the switch to raise the grate.

▶ Return to the boiler door. Note that the red light is now off. Open the door and look inside: A tube or drainage pipe descends through the middle of the floor with a ladder leading down.

▶ Cross the grate and go down into the drain. You will be enveloped in complete darkness. Click five times to see some light ahead. One more click brings you to a ladder leading up. Continue to move

toward the light and emerge from a pipe
high up on a mountainside above the sea.

▶ Turn left and follow a faint, worn path in
the rocks, which goes over the top of the
mountain and down toward the island's
central lake. Move toward a railing on a balcony resting against the side of the cliff and
climb over. Look down and open the round
hatch at your feet. The hatch, locked when
you tried to open it from underneath,
opens to reveal the long, narrow ladder you
climbed earlier that leads to the beach.

▶ Face the cliff and see the double doors. Go
through the doors and into the mountain.
Turn around and deliberately close the
doors, revealing two passageways, one to the
right, the other to the left, that are cunningly hidden when the doors are open. You
will be returning to these doors shortly.

▶ Turn around again and follow the catwalk
into the cave. At the end is an elaborate
trap apparatus used by Gehn for catching
frogs.

▶ Catching a frog is not necessary for win-
ning the game at this point, but if you
want you can return to the beach via the
ladder outside, go to the power control in
the middle of the lake, turn the valve back
to the right, and then return to this chamber. Touch the steel sphere at the top to

open the trap. Click and drag to move one of the tiny food pellets from the open container on the right to the trip lever in the middle of the trap. Throw the lever at the left to lower the trap. After waiting about a minute, throw the lever again and raise the trap. If the trap hasn't closed, lower it again and wait some more. If the trap has closed, touch the top to open it and note the brightly colored frog inside. Listen to its chirp, which is the same as the chirp you heard at the wooden Eye in the frog silhouette on Jungle Island.

▶ While you're here, look up at the fan. The loud clattering sound you hear is the noise of the fan running. The ventilator shaft beyond leads to Gehn's laboratory, but you can't access it while the fan is running.

▶ Go back up the catwalk to the two open passages you found behind the double doors. Go left and follow the steps down to a chamber with another Fire Marble Dome. Go around the side of the dome and note the lens of a kinetoscope set into the side wall of the cavern, which should give you an idea as to where to find it. Look up at the opening in the roof, a geological curiosity that you must remember later.

▶ Close the door to the Fire Marble Dome chamber to reveal another hidden door to the right. Enter this room, find the kinetoscope, and use it to stop the spinning dome. Note the symbol.

▶ Go back up the stairs, and then go straight ahead past the double doors and into the opposite passage. Follow the walkway and emerge on the previously unreachable catwalk above the lake. Go forward until you find a lever and hear the clattering racket of ventilator fans. Throw the lever to turn off the fans.

▶ Continue to follow the catwalk. The front doors to Gehn's laboratory are locked, so continue to follow the catwalk around a curve, and then onto a long, high bridge spanning the gulf from Crater Island back to the Great Golden Dome. When you reach a lever at a raised drawbridge, throw the lever to lower the bridge and open the passage between Crater Island and the Great Golden Dome.

▶ Continue into the dome, and follow the walkway to the left. Pass one open doorway to your left and continue toward the open section of catwalk noted earlier. Turn the large wheel to extend the bridge and complete the walkway back to the Gate Room.

▶ Proceed to the doorway through which you first entered the Golden Dome. Throw the lever handle on the right to raise the end of the bridge between the Gate Room and the Golden Dome to a new position in the dome somewhere above your head. Leave it there—you'll need access to this higher level from the Gate Room later.

▶ Before you return to Crater Island, turn off at the side passage you passed by earlier. It leads to a high catwalk that goes around the outside of the building to the right, but you are stopped by a gap in the walkway. Turn around and press a button on the outer wall to the right of the doorway, and you will see the catwalk restored as the missing section rises into place.

▶ Continue on the path to a heavy door with a lever to the side. Raise the lever to open the door to Position 4 of the Gate Room, the one you couldn't open from the inside before. (This step is not necessary for the game as it has been laid out in this walkthrough, but is presented here for completeness.)

▶ There is one more excursion you can make at this time, and that is to the Temple Island Fire Marble Dome. Head back for the Golden Dome and turn left, following the stairs down to the outer catwalk on the lower level. Stop just before you enter the tunnel and press the button on the wall to your right. You find yourself riding down to a still lower level, where a smooth-walled tunnel leads to a metal stairway heading up to the Fire Marble Dome.

▶ Operate the kinetoscope to determine the yellow symbol associated with this dome, and write it down. You'll need to know it later.

▶ Now return to Crater Island, and go past Gehn's lab, past the switched-off controls for the ventilator fans, and back to the double doors. Go through and down the catwalk straight ahead to the frog-catching chamber. Look up, and then click on the open ventilator duct to climb inside.

Follow the shaft until you reach another ventilator grill, and click on the grating to open it. Drop down into Gehn's laboratory.

► Check out his lab—this is where he conducts experiments to determine the proper kind of wood with which to make paper, the proper beetles to make ink, and all of the other details necessary for creating the books that link among the infinity of worlds. At another table, note the paraphernalia he uses for dissecting the frogs. An extract from the frogs is placed in small, cylindrical containers and smoked in his elaborate pipe.

► Find his lab journal and go through it carefully. Find and record a string of five D'ni numerals. This is the code for opening the inner mechanism of the Fire Marble Domes. At this point, you know the numerals for 1 through 10. You will need to look for patterns within these numerals in order to deduce the translation of any numbers higher than 10.

► Note, incidentally, that this code is different each time you play *Riven*.

- ▶ Note, also, the wooden Eye on the desk with the lab journal and note the symbol on the reverse side. Read the paper underneath it to find out where it came from... and how Gehn found out about it.

- ▶ Examine the stove in the center of the room. Pull the lever to open the door and look inside to see a partly burned linking book. It doesn't work. Note that in Gehn's journal he says he burns books in the oven when they don't work. He seems to be having some trouble getting things right.

- ▶ Go to the front door and open it, unlocking it so it will now open from the outside. Return through the lab, and touch the blue-topped tram-call next to the door. Go to the opposite door and down the steps toward an awaiting tram.

Plateau Island

▶ Ride the tram to Plateau Island. When you arrive, note the door on the opposite side of the tram from the tram's entrance, but don't do anything about it now. Leave the tram, go out the passageway, and climb the steps. Follow the path through some huge, monolithic stones. Approach the titanic building and go up the steps into the portal. Pass the huge, stone plateaus that rise on either side from the surface of a pond. Continue through the crevice in the rock face and enter an elevator.

▶ Turn around, push the button, and go up to the map viewing level. Go forward and look down to the plateaus in the pond you observed earlier, and which are now obviously maps of Riven's five islands.

▶ Look at the control with five buttons shaped like the islands of Riven. Note how pressing one button causes water to flow onto the top of the corresponding island plateau and hump itself into a three-dimensional relief of that island's topography.

▶ Turn around, walk back the way you came all the way through the elevator to another crater lake. In the middle of the lake is a large structure: the Map Room.

▶ Approach the map chamber. As you cross the causeway, look to the left and note the Fire Marble Dome for Plateau Island turning just beyond a narrow, V-shaped cleft in the rock wall of the crater.

▶ Enter the map chamber. Note that the water maps and plateaus outside correspond to the map currently visible here. Press the yellow square to see a 3-D relief map of that one square. Use the handle at the bottom to rotate the 3-D map so that you can view it from all sides.

▶ Each island is divided into squares similar to patterns seen on Temple Island. For example, Crater Island is represented by four squares arranged in a square, while Plateau Island consists of four squares arranged in an "L" shape.

▶ Each square, when you click on it, can be
further divided into a five-by-five square
grid. You need to identify where on each
3-D island map that island's Fire Marble
Dome is located.

▶ In the case of Crater Island, you will have
to use additional clues, since the dome is
underground. Look for the hole or crater
that you saw earlier when you looked up
inside that island's Fire Marble Dome
chamber. The domes on the other islands
are easily identified.

▶ Use the five-by-five grids to create coordinates for each dome site. For example, if
the columns across are labeled **A**, **B**, **C**, **D**,
and **E**, and the rows down are labeled **1**, **2**,
3, **4**, and **5**, then the coordinates of the
dome on Crater Island are B-4. Record all
of the dome sites—or your best guesses—
for later reference.

▶ Leave the map room and go to the junction of catwalks, turning right. Investigate
the dome in the cleft. Note, if you can, the
symbol highlighted in color—a circle with
a horizontal line.

▶ Go back around the catwalk, and follow its
curve counterclockwise. As you walk,
observe the wahrk totems rising from the

lake and note their colors: blue (visible from the side of the lake near the dome), yellow, orange, and green (closest to the kinetoscope).

▶ The kinetoscope is broken, the device pushed out of alignment. To open the dome, simply click your mouse button rapidly until the dome stops rotating.

▶ Return to the elevator, and ride it down to the plateau. Walk along the path, noting the three-dimensional water mountains still rising above the last island you examined. Return to the tram. Rotate the tram to get out on the side of the door you noticed when you first arrived. Go through the door.

▶ Walk down an orange-lit passageway. Note the handle with yellow stripes on the left just before the hexagonal-shaped pool. Throw the lever to raise a golden elevator cage. Go inside. Turn around and push the button to close the elevator and descend beneath the surface of the water.

▶ Emerge from the elevator and follow the passageway through caverns and tunnels. Up ahead, you see Gehn's scribe look up, obviously startled, and dash into a side passage. Follow him to arrive at another tram station, just in time to see the scribe making his escape.

▶ Return to the main passage and turn left. Follow it through a portal and up a long, flight of steps to enter Gehn's underwater Survey Room.

▶ Sit in the throne. Push the button on the control panel to the right to rotate and elevate the throne.

▶ Lower the right-hand lever in front of you to bring down the Color Wheel. Look down at the wheel. Note the symbols, some of which are the same as the symbols you've been noting on each of the Fire Marble Domes. Click on either the symbols or the tabs with finger holes to rotate the wheel. Click on the button at the bottom position to turn on an underwater light.

▶ Go through all of the symbols to connect a specific symbol with a color. The lights are located on the underwater portions of the wahrk totems you noticed earlier. One light, the one symbolized by a circle with a vertical line, is broken; you'll need to guess its color.

▶ The vertical eye shape with a dot, a symbol you've not seen thus far, is blue. The circle with a dot is green. The horizontal eye with a dot in the middle is yellow. The circle with a horizontal line is orange. The eye with a vertically aligned slit pupil is red.

▶ When you click on red, your view shifts up. The red light is visible through the glass of the Viewing Chamber. Wait a few moments to see and hear a live wahrk. Apparently, he's trained to appear to get food when the light is on; when he doesn't get food, he leaves. If you want to play with the wahrk's mind, try calling him three more times and watch him get more agitated each time. After his fourth appearance, he will slam into the glass, and then vanish. He will not reappear unless you return considerably later.

▶ Raise the Color Wheel. Pull the lever to lower the left-hand viewer. This one has only two buttons and six tabs with finger holes. Press the button on the left to see a spy-camera view of Catherine in her prison. When this view is active, the finger hole tabs do nothing.

▶ Press the rightmost button to get a camera's view from Village Lake on Jungle Island. Use the tabs to rotate the view.

▶ Note one view that looks like the silhouette of a fish created by a rock cavern and its reflection in the water, which gives the shape of a delta-wing type configuration. Note a white speck at the pointed end and surmise that the shape is the missing fifth animal silhouette, and that the white speck—unreachable—is the silhouette's wooden Eye.

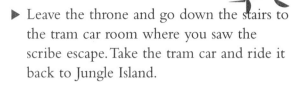

▶ Leave the throne and go down the stairs to the tram car room where you saw the scribe escape. Take the tram car and ride it back to Jungle Island.

The Moiety Age

▶ Leave the tram, go through the open door, and go to the wooden elevator. Ride up one level to the inside of the Jungle Island wahrk idol.

▶ Leave the jungle via the wooden gate and turn right. Follow the wooden catwalk through the blue-lit cavern and out to the lakeside, where a ladder was lowered earlier. Climb up the ladder, go to the prison cell, and go inside. Open the drain grate, pull the ring, open the secret door, and descend into the cavern. Go down the tunnel to the side passage and the room with 25 stones and animal totems.

Touch the stones in the following order: delta-shaped fish, beetle, frog, sunner, and wahrk. This drains the water from the far wall and provides access to the Moiety universe by opening a ledge with an open book. Touch the screen to see the other universe; click to go through. The order is:

Fish   Beetle   Frog   Sunner   Wahrk

- ▶ Enter the room behind you, where a strange idol is on display. Approach the idol to examine it more closely. Quickly turn to see Moiety rebels shoot at you with a blowgun dart.

- ▶ You awake in a boat on the way to a large building that resembles a tree. Explore the room you awake in, and look through a window in a wooden door to see a rebel village. Turn to face the table. A woman, named Nelah, brings you Catherine's journal and your trap book. She mentions Catherine's name, although you cannot understand her language.

- ▶ Examine the journal. Note the entry about a pin that locks the telescope, and find a series of five D'ni numbers. Later, Nelah returns with a linking book. Touch the link image to return to the room with 25 stones.

▶ Leave the Moiety gateway tunnel. If the lights are out, keep clicking to get to the trap door. Pull the ring to exit. Turn right to the end of the catwalk and go down the ladder. Turn around and follow the catwalk into the cavern through the blue-lit cave, and past the jungle and clear-cut area. Return to the tram, which takes you back to Temple Island. Go through the Temple, up the passageway, and across the bridge to the Gate Room.

▶ Push the rotation button to set the door-ways to positions 1 and 3. Go to Position 3, where the ramp beyond now extends upward to a vertical slit high in the Great Golden Dome. Cross the ramp and enter a high, narrow passageway. Note a lever on the wall, and beyond, the Marble Puzzle.

▶ Look at the marble grid. Six marbles are lined up to the right. The grid is a five-by-five array of squares further divided into smaller squares, exactly like the array you saw in the Map Room on Plateau Island.

► Place colored marbles in the appropriate spots, based on what you learned in the Map Room and at the Color Wheel. The color is determined by the symbol that opened each dome. The positions are determined by consulting your notes from your session in the Map Room.

► When you think you have it right, step back and throw the switch on the wall. This lowers the marble press. Push the white button on the wall switch when it appears. An explosion and whooshing sound signals that the marbles are set correctly. You have now powered up the Linking Books in all of the Fire Marble Domes.

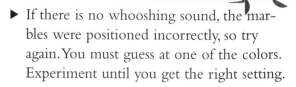

▶ If there is no whooshing sound, the marbles were positioned incorrectly, so try again. You must guess at one of the colors. Experiment until you get the right setting.

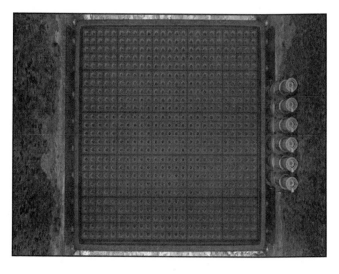

▶ Return to the Gate Room and go to Position 1. Press the rotation button three times to set the gates to Positions 1 and 4.

▶ Go through Position 4 and follow the catwalk beyond. Go into the Golden Dome. Turn left on the catwalk and cross the walkway extension. Pass the entrance to position 3 in the Gate Room and go down the steps to the Golden Dome's lower level catwalk. Exit the door and follow the walkway to the right past the power valve for the West Drawbridge. Stop on a red plate on the path and turn right. Push the button to take the elevator down a level. Turn and follow the tunnel to some steps that lead up. Go up to the Fire Marble Dome.

▶ You now have the five numbers for the dome lock settings from Gehn's lab journal. Move the sliders to the appropriate numbers on the scale and push the button, opening the inner dome and raising the linking book. Open the book and touch the scene inside to travel to Gehn's universe.

Gehn's World

▶ You arrive inside a cage. Note the Linking Books, each with a graphic symbol of a different island. Turn until you see a button on a star-shaped design mounted on the bars. Touch it to call Gehn and have him talk to you. He talks about being in Riven without books, but you know he has been writing books. He tells you that he is a changed man who wants to atone for the trouble he's caused.

- ▶ He also smokes frogs and wears a grand version of the uniform worn by the guard who first greeted you upon your arrival. You know that he uses the wahrks to instill fear in the natives, and—if the elaborate native warning network and Moiety rebellion are any indication—that the natives are, indeed, terrified of him. All suggest that Gehn is not to be trusted.

- ▶ He asks you to go through the trap book first, so he can satisfy himself that it is, indeed, a Linking Book to D'ni. When he holds the trap book in front of you, click on the picture and you'll get trapped inside the book. Watch while Gehn decides to follow you to D'ni. He gets trapped, which frees you, and you are now inside his home outside the cage.

▶ Find the switch that turns on the power to the other Linking Books in the room, and move it to the right.

▶ Find a lever next to a window, and pull it to lower the bars to your former cage.

▶ Find a tunnel leading down a ladder to Gehn's bedroom. Examine the various artifacts in the room. Go to the bedside table and examine his personal journal.

▶ Click on the gray metal sphere on the table, which appears to be some kind of watch. Listen to the sequence of sounds, which are the code to Catherine's prison.

▶ Go back up the ladder to the main room. Go into the cage area. There's a book that links to Prison Island here, the one with a single small square as an identifying graphic. Link to Catherine's island.

Catherine's Prison

▶ You arrive inside the Fire Marble Dome on Catherine's island. Press the button on the floor to the right of the book to lower the book stand and open the dome. Turn and follow the walkway toward a gigantic tree stump covering the entire small, rocky island. Go up the stairs and through a door to an elevator. Note three keys and a lever, plus a pull cord. Press the keys and listen to the different sounds. Enter the correct sequence of sounds (the sequence you heard on the watch in Gehn's bedroom), and then throw the lever to open the cage.

▶ Catherine joins you and pulls the elevator handle to descend. She congratulates you. "We're all free! You captured Gehn!" She tells you to open the fissure and reminds you that the combination is in her journal.

▶ Go back to Gehn's residence. You'll have to stop the dome again because Catherine has just used it.

End Game

▶ In Gehn's home, return to Temple Island by means of the Linking Book. Go through the tunnel to the elevator and press the button to take you up one level. Go through the Golden Dome to the

Gate Room. Go through Position 1 and turn right, going down the stone steps.

▶ Return to the place where you first arrived on the island, at the telescope. Use the code from Catherine's journal to open the hatch. Look through the viewfinder to see stars in the fissure. Pull open the pin that blocks the telescope's descent by clicking on the support strut to the left of the hatch, and then swinging the lever handle up. Step back to the main controls and pull down the lever to the right of the scope. Press the green button.

▶ Repeatedly press the button until the glass breaks.

▶ Now watch Riven destroy itself. Atrus comes through from the chamber in which you first arrived on the island. Catherine arrives a moment later and they embrace; she tells you the villagers are all safely in the Rebel Age. "The path home is now clear for all of us."

▶ Atrus has brought a linking book. Catherine goes through to safety first. He then links through himself, letting the book fall into the fissure. You follow, falling into the Star Fissure… on your way home at last.

Riven: The Lost Episodes

With the help of this game guide, of course, you made it all the way through Riven without a single mistake or wrong turn. Want to see how the game ends if you don't perform so brilliantly?

Restore to a saved game made just *before* the final few moves of play.

You Fail to Trap Gehn

If you fail to trap Gehn before opening the Star Fissure, you lose the game.

You fall into darkness as a world dies.

You Fail to Free Catherine

If you trap Gehn but fail to free Catherine before smashing the glass view port in the Star Fissure, Atrus will come through and take the book. "I don't understand..." He looks at you, bewildered. "You've trapped Gehn, but... why did you signal me? The age is collapsing. There's no time left."

The shock and grief on his face when he realizes that Catherine may be lost forever should spur you on to return to the world of Riven again, this time to end the quest on a less tragic note.

For now, though, the wind howls as a world and a people die.

Make sure you both trap Gehn in the Book *and* release Catherine from her prison, using the code in Gehn's bedroom and you won't have to experience either of these unpleasant endings!

Good luck, and happy adventuring!

APPENDIX A
How It All Came To Be

Long ago, the great civilization of D'ni fell, wrecked by inner discords difficult for outsiders to comprehend. At the height of their power, however, the D'ni had ruled a thousand worlds, worlds that they had built with godlike power and linked to through the creation of their wondrous, half-magical books, a craft perfected by the D'ni across a span of ten thousand years.

Last of the D'ni was Gehn, a child when his world collapsed. When his young wife died years later, he left his newborn son in his mother's care and returned to D'ni's vast caverns and fallen cities. The art of making books and worlds had been lost with civilization's fall, but somehow he would learn the ancient secrets and restore lost D'ni.

For Gehn, it was clear that D'ni's glory could only be restored by the rediscovery of the lost craft of the books, a craft which he could learn only through the painstaking piecing together of scattered, subtle clues and bits of lore sifted from the subterranean ruins of D'ni's fallen, empty cities. Perhaps, in that disconsolate desolation, he went a little mad. Or, perhaps, it was the task he'd set for himself, learning how to write out the description of an entire world, line by line in the peculiarly precise and descriptive vocabularies of the D'ni tongue.

Creating entire worlds…

Eventually, Gehn returned for his son, and together they continued the exploration of D'ni. Atrus learned the craft of writing books from his father. More, he exhibited a talent for writing that far surpassed that of the older man. His rich description, his keen powers of logic and observation, the depth of his understanding and of his abilities to unleash the expressive, creative power of the D'ni script, unveiled worlds utterly beyond the ken of his father. Atrus never presumed to claim he was creating these worlds; nevertheless, it was true that his worlds endured while each of those opened by Gehn sooner or later collapsed.

So it was with the world, or *age* as these book-linked worlds were known, that Gehn called his Fifth Age… the world that would one day be known as Riven.

But it wasn't long before creative differences blossomed into deadly enmity dividing father from son. Atrus could not understand his father's parsimony

of words, the cold and empty leanness of his
descriptive passages, the editorial callousness that
seemed, to Atrus, to all but guarantee each world's
collapse. Worse, to Atrus's mind, was Gehn's over-
weening pride and ambition, which drove him to
abandon whole ages and their innocent inhabitants.
Gehn seemed obsessed with creating more and
more worlds, discarding each in turn when it
proved less than perfect. For him, these worlds and
their populations were his creations, imperfect
sketches to be discarded when they failed to meet
his artistic vision. He was, after all, their god.

For Atrus, however, these ages were pre-existing
worlds, their populations *people*, not failed experiments to be swept away with the rest of the rubbish
when the day's work was done. Atrus had a personal
interest in those people; his wife, Catherine, was
from the Fifth Age. In Atrus's opinion, Gehn's books
were merely means of linking to these new and
pre-existenting worlds and modifying them. But it
seemed that those worlds invaded by Gehn were
inevitably and swiftly doomed by the descriptions
he inserted within their creative matrices.

The Fifth Age—Gehn never bothered to name his
creations, preferring instead to give them only cold
numbers—was a promising world, but like Gehn's
other efforts, the seeds of its destruction were planted
within its heart. Together, Catherine and Atrus decided
to stop Gehn's rape of the worlds, intending to arrange
things so that Riven would become his prison.

Together, they managed to trap Gehn on Riven,
confronting him at the Star Fissure, removing the
last linking book out of that age by dropping it
down that eldritch rift in time and space. Many of

the local Rivenese witnessed that confrontation, when Catherine stepped into another world through a linking book, vanishing like a wraith, and Atrus hurled himself after the book down the fissure. Gehn was, indeed, trapped as Atrus and Catherine had planned.

As a result, the natives learned that Gehn was no god, that Atrus and Catherine had bested him and trapped him in that world. Unfortunately, they leaped to several other, less solid conclusions: Believing that Atrus was a god who had stripped Gehn of his power, that Catherine, a native of Riven, had been chosen by Atrus as his bride, and that she, herself, was transforming into a god who would one day rule Riven forever. From this series of revelations was born the Moiety, dissidents in rebellion against the oppressive and tyrannical rule of Gehn.

The Moiety survived at first in a vast system of interlinking caves beneath the surface of Riven. Eventually, and with Catherine's help when she returned to her native world, the Moiety was able to secure a burned book from Gehn's laboratory, and with this Catherine was able to write the rebels an age of their own, a safe refuge from the tyrant's predations. They adopted a kind of stylized dagger as their emblem; their introduction of these daggers, manufactured in the Moiety Age, puzzled Gehn when he realized that the materials could not be coming from Riven. Catherine, to her dismay, was nothing less than a savior figure, a goddess in her own right come to deliver her people.

The Moiety Age, accessed through secret caverns and by cunningly contrived puzzles, might one day prove to be the salvation of the Rivenese. Unfortunately, before she could carry her plans further, Catherine was captured by Gehn and imprisoned on a tiny island, a fragment of the much larger, original isle of Riven.

Gehn's meddlings were taking their toll, and Riven was disintegrating faster and ever faster. Worse, perhaps, Gehn's tinkering had also changed the infrastructure of Riven to the extent that he could introduce certain key ingredients for his use. For example, a particular species of beetle that provided the necessary dyes for ink, a special type of tree whose pulped wood made paper of the proper fineness, tooth, and texture. He'd written all he needed into Riven; it seemed to enable him to continue his research into creating his own linking books. It took him thirty years, but eventually he did it. After hundreds of trials, after hundreds of failures, Gehn succeeded in creating a new world—his 233rd age—a haven from which he could complete his experiments.

Soon he would be free of crumbling Riven forever.

Atrus, meanwhile, was beset with the problem of what to do about Gehn. Fearing that Catherine was lost on Riven, he could not simply return to that age with a linking book, not if that meant that Gehn might seize the book and use it to effect his own escape. He feared, too, the imminent breakup of Riven, which was accelerating. His efforts were dangerously delayed by the rebellion of his sons, Achenar and Sirrus, in the Myst affair. Carried away by megalomania and greed (had they been touched by the disease of Atrus's father as well?), they trapped Atrus in D'ni, leaving him helpless, save for the writings with which he could implement certain changes in dying Riven.

Working furiously for many months, he managed to write those changes into Riven's matrix, slowing the destruction, but he knew with cold certainty that the final Armageddon of that age could not be long deferred. He could not observe the changes directly from his prison within D'ni, but he could note them on a fundamental level and understand that there was now no way the decay could ever be reversed. Catherine might well be doomed, and all of the inhabitants of Riven as well.

And then... a miracle. Someone, a stranger from another world, another *reality* beyond the Star Fissure, found the lost Myst book, used it to go through to the Isle of Myst, and, ultimately, managed to free Atrus from his prison on D'ni. The stranger seemed willing to help with the problem of Riven, although what he was being asked to do was extraordinarily dangerous.

Atrus would send the stranger into Riven carrying only a specially designed trap book, one that would appear to be a linking book back to D'ni. Atrus knew that Gehn could scarcely resist such a temptation—a means of escaping from Riven once and for all! Once the stranger had trapped Gehn, he would send a signal which would summon Atrus, bringing a real linking book to D'ni.

The stranger agreed.

And with this acceptance began the final chapter of the saga of Riven.

APPENDIX B
Worlds For The Making

An infinity of worlds… literally, worlds without end.

This is the promise of Riven, where books describing worlds create links to alternate realities, places, worlds, *ages* where people and life and even physical laws might be quite different than the mundane reality we know as Earth.

Purest fantasy, of course.

Or… is it?

Since the end of the nineteenth century, physics—the means by which we apprehend the cosmos and the laws that govern it—has been undergoing revolution upon stunning revolution, until all that is clear is J.B.S. Haldane's maxim that the universe is not only stranger than we imagine, it is stranger than we *can* imagine. That peculiarly twisty pocket of physics known as quantum mechanics arose from the discovery of the dual nature of light, packets of energy, or *quanta*, that can at one and the same time behave both as electromagnetic waves and as discrete particles. Physicist Werner Heisenberg went from there to the formulation of what came to be known as Heisenberg's Uncertainty Principle, which states that it is impossible to know both the position and the momentum of a subatomic particle without changing one or the other. In fact, the introduction of observation changes the very phenomena under observation; this so-called observer effect predicts that we help shape the universe simply by living here.

Such arrogance! To actually suggest that the existence of the universe, born of the "Big Bang" Theory billions of years before life or worlds evolved from its fires of energy and chaos, is dependent on the minds of humans or others to somehow will it into being smacks of nothing so much as a kind of megalomaniacal hubris, an arrogant, doomed assumption by Man of the prerogatives of God.

And yet, this seems to be precisely the way things work, as validated both by the mathematics of quantum mechanics, and by experimental results.

Erwin Schroedinger illuminated this radical, seemingly mystical notion by inventing a thought experiment, a well-known physical parable that today bears the name Schroedinger's Cat. Suppose, the parable goes, an experimenter places a live cat in a sealed box. With the cat is a vial of prussic acid, designed to be broken if and only if some random event—say, the decay of a given radioactive particle with a half-life of one hour—occurs.

The cat has a fifty-fifty chance of surviving the hour. At the end of sixty minutes, the experimenter opens the box. Will he find a live cat… or a dead one? More to the point, is the cat alive or dead *before the experimenter opens the box?*

According to one of the weirder interpretations of quantum theory, the correct answer is "yes." Until the box is open, say the equations, and the so-called "observer effect" comes into play, the cat is both alive and dead, a kind of mathematical wave function that does not, that *cannot*, collapse into one probability or the other until the cat's state is actually observed.

The discussion seems to fly in the face of reason. However, though this would hardly be the first time that insights into the way the universe works seemed to defy common sense. In fact, enough experimental evidence has accumulated since Heisenberg's day to suggest that quantum physics does, in fact, provide the best interpretation of how the universe—or the *universes*—actually work. One explanation—known as the Copenhagen Interpretation—postulates that every time a quantum event occurs (an electron goes up an energy level, its spin changes, it loses energy), a new universe branches off to accommodate the change.

This theory is controversial to say the least. Can it be that a new universe is born *each and every time* something as insubstantial as a photon is born, or the spin-state of an electron changes?

Perhaps nature is not so profligate. Perhaps the multiplicity of universes overlap somehow, in ways we cannot yet understand. Perhaps such overlappings explain how people could unknowingly step from one world to another, as seems to have happened upon occasion. The accounts of Charles Forte and of other books are filled with the names and descriptions of mysterious vanishings and arrivals—Kaspar Hauser, Judge Crater, the two women at the Garden of Triannon, the green children of Suffolk, the crew of the Marie Celeste, the ubiquitous "Grays" who *could* be extraterrestrial but who can exhibit powers more easily explained by extradimensional origins—and so very many more.

Even so, it seems that nothing less than an infinity of parallel universes, alternate realities distinct from one another yet ever splitting one from another like the branches of a tree, could embrace so bizarre a concept.

Infinity is a very *large* number, one that means that *anything* is possible—somewhere. An infinity of universes means that somewhere, somehow, every possible event or combination of events has taken place. Every alternate history ever imagined, every world of fantasy ever dreamed of, every universe conceived by every writer of science fiction, every hallucination spawned by every madman, all, *all* have concrete reality, somewhere. Did they exist from the beginning, or were they somehow created by the very act of thinking about them? The question may well be meaningless; time may be an illusion from the unique perspective of the metacosmos, and reality may require no more than *belief* to give it substance.

The Nobel-winning physicist Niels Bohr once commented, "Those who are not shocked when they first come across quantum theory cannot possibly have understood it."

In Riven, of course, the ancient D'ni learned to write books—using special papers, special inks, even a special and highly descriptive language—that allowed adepts among the people to cross over to other worlds. Or were they, in fact, creating those worlds? The concept hangs upon the space-twisting horns of the Copenhagen Interpretation.

And more…

Consider. Within the framework of quantum physics and the Worlds of If, it is quite possible—more, it is certain—that somewhere, some*when*, universes exist—infinities of them, in fact, where magic works. Where Sauron's minions seek the One Ring, and hobbits shun such inconvenient things as adventures. Where the Lensman battles the evil forces of dark Eddore, or where crystal cities gleam along the banks of the Grand Canal on Mars. Where Vikings colonized all of North America, or perhaps where the cause of Southern Independence was won at Gettysburg. Where *you* are president of the United States of Columbia… or Emperor of the Earth and all her far-flung colonies.

And worlds exist where books link world to world, where imagination creates entire ages, where the surface tension of water enables it to be sculpted like clay, where Catherine and Atrus struggle to stop the final collapse of Riven.

And where *you* arrive on a small and rocky island to find the fate of the Riven Age in your hands…

From the pages of a mythic book
comes a tale of a forgotten land

MYST

The Book of the Black Ships

a graphic adventure from the
Mechanical Age . . .

available at a comic-book store near you

To find your local comic-book store,
call 1-888-COMIC-BOOK